REMEMBER
and Perish Not

ANITA R. CANFIELD

BOOKCRAFT
Salt Lake City, Utah

Library of Congress Catalog Card Number 98-70867
ISBN 1-57008-420-3

First Printing, 1998

Printed in the United States of America

CONTENTS

$\mathcal{T}$HANKSGIVING FOR MEMORIES

Some of you have shared your most painful memories with me. We could, collectively, fill volumes with our shared sorrows. It is certain we could list some of the greatest tribulations known to man. If you were to spend the next five minutes in silence and choose the most painful memory to ponder, five minutes from now there would be a great number of visible tears.

My saddest memories number with yours, and some are difficult to think about indeed. With a few reflective moments I can summon tender feelings as I ponder past sorrows.

Memory is a two-edged sword. One side is a ragged edged weapon that inflicts distressing thoughts that may continue to wound the soul.

But the words here are about the other side of memory: the side of exquisite sharpness that slices through anguish and mistakes and cuts away the decay of forgetfulness to reveal soul-warming comfort and hope.

I am an ordinary woman. I do not possess exclusive information on overcoming the world. My witness is borne from experience, from trials and constant mistakes, from struggling to lift that two-edged sword and discovering there is always one, *even the Savior,* who is there to help me lift it, even to lift it for me, if I am willing.

The world was saddened to learn that an honored statesman and former United States president was afflicted with Alzheimer's disease, a cruel thief that would eventually rob him of his precious memories. Renewed global attention was given to the sadness and suffering of many families whose loved ones have simply disappeared while yet alive.

Memory is a precious commodity. It is the springboard for feelings of joy and sorrow and for expressions of emotion.

Memory is the tender core of poetry, song, anthems, and other venues that stir us emotionally.

Memory produces spiritual threads that bind parent to child, child to family, family to generation, and generations to humanity. It is memory that binds humanity to God as Alma expressed to his son Helaman: "It has hitherto been wisdom in God that these things should be preserved; for behold, they have enlarged the memory of this people, yea, and convinced many of the error of their ways, and brought them to the knowledge of their God unto the salvation of their souls" (Alma 37:8).

Memory is so valued that we find blank bound-together pages being sold in retail stores as journals. We find businesses dedicated solely to the printing of slides, photographs, and videos. We find treasures assembled in vast buildings called museums and records safeguarded in vaults called archives. We find tributes of remembrance in places we visit called memorials.

Careers have been made, even fortunes lost and won, on what we call memory.

Memory—without it we become detached, disengaged, disconnected with all of our experiences.

Where would you be right now without your memories?

Think of the anniversaries, the birthdays, the first date, the first kiss, the first dance, school celebrations and graduations, family reunions, funerals, and other such events now long gone.

Our children love to have us take out the family slides and spend an evening going back through the years. They always share the same stories and laugh at the same memories, but they never seem to tire of it.

Our adopted daughter at about age eight or nine began to struggle with questions about whether or not she was really part of our family. My husband felt inspired to bring out the slides of her life. We gathered around her, and each family member shared, slide by slide, memories of her arrival and development over the years. There were great stories of tenderness and humorous ones that made everyone laugh. We watched her absorb the comfort as she viewed and heard of the love and desire for her to be included in our family.

Shortly before my husband's mother, Viola, passed away, she distributed some of her humble earthly treasures to her posterity. She gave this task her deepest love. She thought about each family member and then carefully selected something she believed that person would really enjoy. She gave to me her own mother's cameo. Her mother died when Viola was only a child, six years old. She had very little memory left of this mother she had so often longed for. The cameo was one of her dearest possessions. These people came from humble means, and the cameo probably isn't of much monetary value. I don't want to know it's earthly value, because to me it is priceless; it is a memory of Viola.

How important is it that we are able to remember?

The last evening of the 1995 Sandstone Las Vegas, Nevada Stake Girls' Camp the young women assembled at the amphitheater. Each received a blindfold and was asked to place it over her eyes and not remove it until she was told to do so.

They were also asked not to speak or ask any questions throughout the entire activity. Then they were escorted through the forest in groups of ten to fifteen by various adult leaders. They were lead first to the feet of "Nephi" and listened to his instructions. Then on to "Mary," "Jesus," and "President Ezra Taft Benson." Each of the readers who portrayed these individuals gave the "blind" women special instructions—through scripture and counsel—that would enable them to get back to the presence of God.

Since they had no sight they moved slowly and awkwardly from messenger to messenger, always aided by the adult leaders. Some girls stumbled, some stubbed toes and ran into rocks and bushes. Others got swatted by hanging branches or scratched by brushing against tree bark. Several times, because they were holding hands, one teetering girl would cause several others to fall down as well. But they all finished the course.

One by one they were then led to the top of a small hill where the end of a thick rope had been tied to the trunk of a large tree. The rope was stretched down the hill about three hundred feet and was held tightly in place by adults at the other end. A large knot in the rope had been placed near the end, about twenty feet from the finish.

As each girl took her turn at the top of the rope, she was given only one instruction: no matter what happens, never let go of the rope!

Unknown to the girls were the people stationed at various intervals along the path. Those on the far side of the rope were encouraging them and reminding them to hold on. Others on the side of the rope tried to persuade them to let go. They were gifted in how persuasive they were!

I watched some of these adults slip an arm around a shoulder and say, "You did a great job, this is the end, come with me."

Many let go, innocently going with a trusted voice. Those who let go were taken back to the top where they were taught a small sermon on repentance by a member of the stake presidency and sent back to try again.

Some girls left the rope three and four times, some only once, others held fast to the very end. The big knot near the end did fool many, it really did seem like the end. Twenty feet left to go and here they were persuaded to let go and they had to start over.

Eventually all of them realized which voices to listen to and they all made it to the end. And what of the end? As each girl completed the journey, they were wrapped in the welcoming arms of a loving leader who whispered, "Well done, thou good and faithful servant! You made it!" Then this leader would escort the girl back to her seat. When all the girls were seated the blindfolds were removed, and there in the midst of that dark forest was an enormous, ancient tree, strung with hundreds of white lights, making the darkness shiver with it's luminosity—a glorious vision of eternity, with a gift on it's branches for each girl.

This exercise was a vivid, symbolic portrayal of our journey here in mortal life. We receive instructions through the prophets and scriptures to help us hold to the rod. We fall and get scratched and bruised and have to repent again and again. The rod is always there, it never moves, we are the ones who move away from it. There are voices of temptation. There are voices we can truly trust. We must listen with spiritual eyes and ears because physical sight is sometimes blinded by distractions.

The most significance in all of this came from the words of the girls themselves during the testimony meeting that followed. They concluded that they were able to hold fast only because they *remembered* what had been said to them by the instructors in the forest and the person at the top who told them that no matter what happens, never let go of the rope!

One little girl, who had been persuaded to let go of the rope five times stood and described how she was confused and didn't really catch on to what was happening. The success

she finally had was because she began to ponder and to remember all of what had been said.

I wish you could have seen her the last time down. Like a
bullet she went, holding fast, literally pushing away the
tempters, and when she reached the knot, she felt over it with
confident hands and hung on and pushed to the end. In the
arms of a loving leader she broke down, at last releasing endless tears that fell softly on the forest floor.

We stand here in the last decade of this century, we stand
on the threshold of a new century. I also believe we stand
somewhere near the door of the Millennium. We have witnessed in the past months and years spectacular global events,
events that are preparing the idle fields of the earth for a massive sowing of the seeds of the gospel of Jesus Christ around
the entire world. How great will be the harvest!

The gates of eternity are opening. Hope is the key that has
opened them. Faith and obedience is the chariot that will
carry us through them.

As times become more perilous, and the world appears
more hopeless, many are holding fast to the iron rod. But
some, even great and noble ones, are beginning to let go; and
not all are being tempted away in sins of commission. Many
are being tempted away with sins of omission.

There are some of us who will let go because we would
allow spiritual priorities to become tangled in the network of
worldly pursuits. Some will leave the path because it seems too
difficult. Some will claim that the reach for perfection is un-
attainable, or that it puts too much pressure on us. There will
be others who might be persuaded away from basic doctrines
by worldly philosophies that refute even things like the Word
of Wisdom or honoring and sustaining the laws of our land.
Others might begin to believe they know better than the
Lord's servants, his prophets. Some will let go because they
have been offended. Many will let go because they feel such a
lack of self-esteem because they perceive that everyone at

church seems to have a life in order except them. And many, many more will let go because they simply lose their memory—they forget—they fail to remember.

I visited with a stake president who told me of an experience with a couple, who, having let go of the rod, were already fast progressing down one of the darker side roads. As they left his office one evening he lingered at his desk, pondering this couple's compiling mountain of problems over the past months. He began to realize that the trial that had started all of this rebelliousness was almost identical to a trial he and his wife had faced many years earlier. Indeed, he realized that many of the problems he had seen as a bishop and as a stake president were not unlike his own trials and challenges, and he wondered in amazement what was so different about him, that had enabled him to overcome the tests and remain full of hope, holding fast to the rod.

His mind began to go back through time, trial after trial, experience after experience, injustice after injustice, sorrow after sorrow, hardship after hardship, failure after failure. He walked the years, he remembered the pain. And then, as if a light went on he suddenly knew what the difference had been!

He was no more capable than another. He had not been given less or more than most. He did not possess some unusual extra power of endurance. He had simply chosen to *remember.*

In the dark midnight of his heartaches, instead of letting go because he could not see, he held fast by remembering the goodness of the Lord to him. When only thoughts of despair pressed in upon him, he would dispel those thoughts by sorting in his mind the times he did feel the Spirit, by remembering the moments of comfort, moments of joy, moments of peace. He focused on his testimony, even bearing it to himself and on his knees to his Father in Heaven. And thus, over the years of his life he had been able to remove mountains of doubt by remembering and counting his blessings.

If ever there was a need, these are days for remembering.

This great evil now upon the face of the whole world seeks to destroy our memory. Forgetfulness creates faithlessness and faithlessness begets hopelessness. There is a lesson and a warning laced among the scriptures that tells us we must deliberately cultivate memory: "How is it that ye have forgotten what great things the Lord has done for us? . . . How is it that ye have forgotten that the Lord is able to do all things according to his will, for the children of men, if it so be that they exercise faith in him?" (1 Nephi 7:11–12.)

This powerful word *remember* is a great handgrip for us if we recognize it's significance in the scriptures. Perhaps the Lord has used it purposefully in his instruction so that not only will we be able to better hold to the rod, but so that we will never let go of it!

Remember and all the words that match it—memory, mind, thought, think, ponder, meditate, forget, forgotten—help us understand that we must be responsible enough to develop this spiritual ability for ourselves.

"Even so I would that ye should remember, and always retain in remembrance, the greatness of God" (Mosiah 4:11).

"Remember the words of your God; pray unto him continually by day, and give thanks unto his holy name by night" (2 Nephi 9:52).

"And I, Nephi, have written these things unto my people, that perhaps I might persuade them that they would remember the Lord their Redeemer" (1 Nephi 19:18).

"Seeing that our merciful God has given us so great knowledge concerning these things, let us remember him, and lay aside our sins, and not hang down our heads, for we are not cast off. . . . [the Lord] remembereth us also. Therefore, cheer up your hearts, and remember that ye are free to act for yourselves—to choose the way of everlasting death or the way of eternal life." (2 Nephi 10:20, 22–23.)

"And again, when they thought of the immediate goodness of God, and his power in delivering Alma and his brethren out of the hands of the Lamanites and of bondage, they did raise their voices and give thanks to God" (Mosiah 25:10).

"Now my son, I would that ye should repent and forsake your sins. . . . Oh, remember, and take it upon you, and cross yourself in these things. . . . And now, my son, this was the ministry unto which ye were called, to declare these glad tidings unto this people, to prepare their minds; or rather that salvation might come unto them, that they may prepare the minds of their children to hear the word at the time of his coming." (Alma 39:9, 16.)

We must deliberately cultivate memory. Without remembering, we have the tendency to be selfish, to murmur, to become weak and fainthearted, to become faithless and hopeless. Just the simple act of changing thoughts can change feelings. If our feelings are changed, our behavior follows right along. Without remembering the covenants we have made to consecrate our time, talents, and resources to the building up of the kingdom, many of us will begin to murmur and criticize Church leaders. Without remembering spiritual experiences of comfort and joy, we will become so fainthearted and weak that when trials beset us, they will overcome us. Without remembering our testimonies and bearing them, we will become faithless. And without remembering the Savior and the Atonement and not only what he did for us but why, we will become hopeless.

Cultivating memory is impossible without counting our blessings.

There is a principle of art and design called *variety in harmony*. It means to bring together many different elements such as line, color, texture, and shape and combine them to blend harmoniously with each other. It takes practice and skill to learn how to create personality and uniqueness in each separate room of the house and yet have all the rooms be in harmony with one another.

Variety in harmony is how we live among people who share

our beliefs and people who do not. It is how we can be happy day to day even if many of those days are filled with problems and disappointments. It is how we can feel undiminished among people who have more talent than we do and humbled among those who have less. It is how we can live with family members who have individual personalities and strengths and weaknesses, but still feel we are united as one.

Variety in harmony, however, is impossible to achieve without gratitude. Whenever I am out of harmony with my work, my husband, my family, or the Lord, I can always look to one source: the level of my gratitude.

Some years ago my husband and I had the opportunity to take our children for a visit to England and Germany. I had been very specific to the travel agent about our accommodations. Many seasoned travelers had given me their recommendations to ensure a stressless vacation.

When we arrived at our first hotel it was not what we had requested. It was dark and damp and extremely shabby. We piled into two taxis and began hotel hopping until we found one that pleased the eye and the budget.

This same scene occurred at the next destination and the next one after that. When we arrived about a week later at the fourth place, my family groaned as we tramped down the hall to see the rooms. Key in hand, I opened the door and everyone followed behind. Immediately I began to complain and criticize the amenities.

My then nineteen-year-old daughter began to speak.

"Mom, I think this is a great room. I can't believe I'm even here in this beautiful country. I feel so lucky to be able to come here, and with all of you to be here with me. This is a beautiful room. I never dreamed of being in a foreign country and I'm so glad to have some place like this to stay."

She spoke the truth, and it was like someone had performed spiritual surgery on my heart in a moment. I could hardly wait to find time alone to repent and express those same words of gratitude to the Lord. What a shift occurred in my behavior after my thoughts were changed!

After my friend lost her husband to a heart attack, she spoke to me of gratitude. She said she often complained because his shoes weren't put away. Now she was so grateful to have had those shoes in her life.

Another friend shared a story with me about a woman who had been injured permanently in a terrible hunting accident. She had been shot in the back and left hopelessly paralyzed from the chest down. Although she had use of her arms, her body had been damaged so severely that she was forced to remain in bed for the rest of her life.

My friend was a member of this woman's ward at the time of the accident. She spent many hours at the side of her bed bringing news and good cheer. However, my friend related to me, with a certain wonder in her voice, that she never left that home without having been inspired and uplifted by this paralyzed woman's gentle, unwavering spirit.

Not more than five years later, this tender sister's frail body could no longer do battle against the raging onslaught of her paralysis and she quietly passed away.

During the course of these five years, the ward had been divided and families had moved in and out. This bedridden sister had sadly not been able to be a part of all this change, and my friend was afraid there would be a pitifully small showing at the funeral. She decided to arrive twenty minutes early with her family to help fill the chapel and hopefully bring some comfort to the grieving family.

She arrived early and found the parking lot nearly full. When she walked in she found the chapel already brimming over with people. There were men in the cultural hall scrambling to set up chairs for the seemingly endless flow of people who were still coming in. And they kept coming in, right up until the time the service was to start. They filled the chapel, the cultural hall, overflow rooms, and even the foyer! There were more people assembled there than at most stake conferences!

It was during the funeral as the talks were given and love expressed that the congregation learned of this good and noble woman's life. After the accident she was overwhelmed with emotional pain and imprisoned by fear. As she lay bedridden, trapped by these thoughts day after day and week after week, she was flooded with a sense of utter emptiness. Until at last, unable to bear the emptiness any longer, she began to fill her mind with thoughts and memories of when she felt complete and overflowing with life. *She began to remember.* It was during these hours that her life truly changed. Her fullness of life had nothing to do with her ability to walk and move around. She began to remember what did. She remembered that it was her love and service for others that made her feel whole. She could do that standing or lying down. She began to remember other blessings, other good and bounteous gifts. She remembered again the good things of the earth that were hers. For the next five years she immersed herself in serving and loving others from her hospital bed at home through phone calls, cards, letters, homemade gifts, and an ever-listening ear. The assembled mourners were a testimony to her cheerful and grateful life. All present that day were witnesses to her unfaltering grip on the rod.

This could have been a different story with a different ending. If she had allowed her original feelings to remain unchecked she would have led a different life. But by remembering her blessings she changed her thoughts; her behavior changed.

Gratitude is a measuring stick of our spirituality. A grateful heart is a humble heart. What do you think is the first emotion you will feel when you see the Savior when he comes again? I think it will be an overwhelming, joyous gratitude.

A grateful heart is a humble heart. A humble heart is generous and unselfish. It has been said that the sin of ingratitude is more serious that the sin of revenge. With revenge we return evil for evil, but with ingratitude we return evil for good.

In her book *Lighten Up!* Chieko Okazaki summarizes the deepening of spiritual maturity through gratitude:

Whenever anyone gave us a gift—and our Japanese and Hawaiian neighbors were always generous with what little they had—my mother taught me to return the plate, clean and polished, and bear another gift in return. The size of the gift was not important. She would say, "We must return something, if only a box of matches." Little boxes of wooden matches sold for a penny when I was a girl. It was not a feeling of paying something back in kind, in the sense of purchasing a service or giving someone a wage. Instead, it was a recognition of a reciprocal relationship of giving and taking. I remember my mother would say, *"On gaeshi."* Those words do not mean "Be grateful," or "Return the favor," but rather, "Acknowledge the obligation," with even a little sense of *"Honor* the obligation." When I first read the Book of Mormon, I understood this feeling of *"on gaeshi"* when I read King Benjamin's sermon:

"For behold, are we not all beggars? Do we not all depend upon the same Being, even God, for all the substance which we have, for both food and raiment, and for gold, and for silver, and for all the riches which we have of every kind?

"And behold, even at this time, ye have been calling on his name, and begging for a remission of your sins. And has he suffered that ye have begged in vain? Nay; he has poured out his Spirit upon you, and has caused that your hearts should be filled with joy, and has caused that your mouths should be stopped that ye could not find utterance, so exceedingly great was your joy." (Mosiah 4:19–20.)

Many of us know that someone has made *zori* for us at fifty cents a pair. We attend schools we did not build. We read books we did not print. We wear clothes that someone else sewed for us. We eat food that someone else grew for us. Many times, we spend money that we did not earn personally. We learn the gospel from teachers who have prepared themselves for our sake. It is a sign of spiritual maturity, I think, to acknowledge that our acceptance of these gifts brings an obligation upon us. There are people to whom we should express appreciation for sacrifices. There are reverent ways in which we should use natural resources, consider the contributions of others, honor those who have gone before.

To acknowledge our dependence, our debt, our relationship to God and to one another does not make us powerless or weak. Rather, it is a relationship of great joy, as King Benjamin has described, of appreciation for the sacrifice, of love, and of gratitude. Whatever we can return is not payment for that sacrifice, but rather a joyful acknowledgment of our relationship and the ties that bind us together. (Salt Lake City: Deseret Book Co., 1993, pp. 31–32.)

Gratitude is such a pure form of remembering. It helps us purge out selfishness and self-centeredness. Gratitude sustains us during times of spiritual famine and great trials of faith. Counting our blessings instead of our sorrows can help us change our thoughts from those that will lead us to perish to those that will see us victorious.

My mother's patriarchal blessing contains a powerful promise to her posterity that when they are called to fight the battles of life they will be victorious. The fastest way to victory is through increased gratitude, which makes us more humble, more meek, more submissive. As we pick up the swords of battle, there will be time for rest. The "rest" does not mean freedom from the fight, it means a moment to gather strength. It is in these moments that our memories need to recall the goodness of God in our lives. Then we, as Coriantumr, will lean on our swords to rest a while, and then rise to fight again (see Ether 15:30).

I remember meeting a sister in Oregon some years ago who told me of her experience through months of extreme financial and emotional hardship. Then, even physical illness was added to her burdens. One day she was evidently pondering her situation, probably with much sorrow and weeping and questioning posed to the Lord. With a hint of regret in her voice, she admitted her main question to him had been The One. You know which one, the one laced with self-pity, "Why is this happening to me?"

She asked it first in self-pity and then with *real intent,* "Why is this happening, Lord?"

The answer she received was loud and clear and not at all what she expected. It was a simple sentence, "Victoria, count your blessings." And it startled her. There was a sure conviction of the Lord's confidence in her in the message. She got up, took out some paper, and began to count her blessings. She wrote word after word, line after line, until the words multiplied into pages. She began to *remember* the Lord's goodness to her. Gratitude overwhelmed her. The gravity of her situation seemed so much more diminished, and the hard edges of her pain began to soften and disappear. Pain was definitely reduced.

Try a simple exercise and write down the following:

1. Something your physical body can do that you are grateful for
2. Something beautiful you saw in nature today
3. Something about your present Church assignment that has blessed you
4. Something unique that you love in one of your family members
5. Something someone has done for you that has uplifted you
6. Something you learned from adversity or inspiration that came in a time of need
7. An act of service you gave that strengthened you, the giver

Now, tonight or later today, expand each of these seven areas by adding six more related examples under each one. That will give you forty-two memories to ponder. Then, mention some of these as you pray tonight and feel the power you have as you speak gratitude to the Lord.

A "mind hardened in pride" (Daniel 5:20) will fail to remember to be grateful. It takes humility to "putteth off the natural man" (Mosiah 3:19) who is far from being full of grateful memories.

Selfishness causes us to withhold giving praise and support

to another. Selfishness makes it easier to lie if it serves our purpose or eases our personal accountability. Selfishness indulges us in our hobbies, talents, and careers while neglecting others and the Lord's work. Selfishness applauds our own accomplishments and flaunts them insensitively in front of others. Selfishness finds delight in others' failures and is jealous of others' successes. Selfishness deals dishonestly with our fellowmen. Selfishness causes dishonor among family members and loved ones, even neglect of parents. Selfishness encourages us to be offended, to exaggerate our own sufferings and disappointments, to become inconsolable in discouragement, and to give up serving others because we feel neglected or lonely. Selfishness causes adultery, fornication, and other sexual sins. Selfishness seeks rewards for self in place of giving the gifts of tithes and offerings, or of keeping the Sabbath day holy.

Perhaps in the same way, although seemingly much more insignificant, is an ungrateful heart that demonstrates selfishness by not returning in excellent condition that which has been borrowed. Or what about the ungrateful heart that won't fulfill a Church assignment or responsibility because it has too much to do? Or what about the selfishness expressed when we refuse a Church calling altogether because it won't fit into our current schedule? What about the beautiful sunset we feasted upon that we never bothered to say thank you for? or the difficulties and problems that were solved through direct inspiration from the Lord and yet, when over, were forgotten with ingratitude.

"Yea, and we may see at the very time when he doth prosper his people, yea, in the increase of their fields, their flocks and their herds, and in gold, and in silver, and in all manner of precious things of every kind and art; sprang their lives, and delivering them out of the hands of their enemies; softening the hearts of their enemies that they should not declare wars against them; yea, and in fine, doing all things for the welfare and happiness of his people; yea, then is the time that they do harden their hearts, and do forget the Lord their God" (Helaman 12:2).

Remembering the generosity of others helps us remember God's generosity to us. Remembering all the times others have served us in or out of Church callings and assignments or blessed our loved ones' lives, helps us remember that we too must serve. Remembering the beauties of this earth helps us remember the joy and goodness in being alive and that God wants us to be happy. Remembering past difficulties and the inspiration that came in those moments of need helps us remember that we can be more humble. By changing thoughts, we can change our behavior.

The proud do not want to remember. Pride keeps our memories insulated. The proud murmur. Murmuring turns to criticism. The critical and murmuring heart is often unteachable and unreachable. And certainly a murmuring heart is an ungrateful one.

Remember Laman and Lemuel? Look at the great spiritual experiences they had—angels, a brother filled with the Spirit, Laban delivered into their hands, a Liahona, and on and on—yet, they refused to remember these things. Instead of remembering, and remembering with gratitude, they murmured, criticized, became unteachable, and found themselves outside the membership of the Church. The guilty take the truth hard.

"And it came to pass that I said unto them that I knew that I had spoken hard things against the wicked, according to the truth; and the righteous have I justified, and testified that they should be lifted up at the last day; wherefore, the guilty taketh the truth to be hard, for it cutteth them to the very center. And now my brethren, if ye were righteous and were willing to hearken to the truth, and give heed unto it, that ye might walk uprightly before God, then ye would not murmur because of the truth, and say: Thou speakest hard things against us." (1 Nephi 16:2–3.)

"And ye have murmured because he hath been plain unto

you. Ye say that he hath used sharpness; ye say that he hath been angry with you; but behold, his sharpness was the sharpness of the power of the word of God, which was in him; and that which ye call anger was the truth." (2 Nephi 1:26.)

I sat next to a former general Primary president of the Church in the cultural hall at the dinner before the keynote address of a women's conference. She was there because she was the wife of the president of that particular mission, and I was there as the keynote speaker. This had not been the first time we had been together on a program. It was good to see her and feel the strength of her spirit.

Their mission was coming to an end in a few months. Her husband had been summoned to return to the Missionary Training Center for a meeting about the change of presidency. The day he was to report to Provo was also the day of their son's graduation from the University of Utah.

They realized that if he took an earlier flight, he could arrive in Salt Lake City in time for the morning graduation and have plenty of time before his scheduled afternoon meeting at the Missionary Training Center. He called the presiding authority over his area and told him of the plans. He was told that he would not receive permission to do this. He was to take the scheduled flight and report directly to the Missionary Training Center.

As I listened to this valiant woman, I could sense the struggle it had been for them. She could have said, "Can you believe that, Anita, only a few hours and forty miles, what difference would it make?" If she had said that then this story also might have had a different ending.

But that is not what she said. She said: "Anita, it was *hard,* but we decided we are on a mission. This is what we told the Lord we would do for three years. We are missionaries for the Lord. We are glad to serve. We are glad to be able to do our part. We are glad to do exactly what is asked of us."

No murmuring word escaped her tongue. They remem-

bered who they were and where they were and why they were
there. I have no doubts of the firmness of their grip on the
rod.

As we serve in the kingdom under the leadership of others, we raise our hands in agreement to sustain and support
our Church leaders. These are men and women of vast ability
and also of vast weakness. Neither really matters when it
comes to our part in sustaining those leaders. Our responsibility is to remember the gospel is not a competition of heart,
might, mind, and strength. It is a school where we learn to
surrender the heart, might, mind, and strength to the Lord. It
really doesn't matter whether the bishop or the road show director or the sacrament bread coordinator does his job with
all the finesse, skill, knowledge, and expertise of a corporate
officer. What does matter is that we, who serve under them or
with them, overlook their imperfections and refrain from
murmuring. We don't have all the information and inspiration necessary to make as proper a judgment as does the person who wears the mantle of their calling.

Murmurers don't murmur in solitude. They murmur out
loud to any available ear. Murmuring can be contagious—
worse, murmuring can create "camps." Remember Thomas B.
Marsh's wife? She murmured over a pint of cream she said be-
longed to her and not her neighbor. She murmured to Elder
Marsh. She was angry and she wanted him to be angry. That
wasn't enough so they murmured to others. They wanted to
be justified, to be supported. Their murmuring became
anger. That anger consumed them and led them through a
list of Church authorities in their relentless search for justification of that anger and eventually out the back door of the
Church. Murmuring eventually cost them their membership.
They let go of the rod.

The danger with a "camp" is that after we express murmuring to seek justification for ourselves and to be correct in
front of a crowd, it is very difficult to turn around and admit
we were wrong in front of that crowd. It is so much easier to

be wrong just in front of the Lord! Humility works wonders and helps us respond quickly, before our hearts harden and we suddenly find it much harder to repent and change our attitude.

Remembering our covenants of consecration helps us concentrate on our responsibilities in the kingdom and not worry about those of another. Remembering our covenants of consecration will enable us to hold fast to the rod when great obligations or challenges are required of us. Sometimes those obligations and challenges are financial, sometimes physical, sometimes emotional, but always they are part of the promises we have made to the Lord.

If we choose to murmur over what is asked of us, we will find it very difficult to remember. Murmuring requires the mouth to move. When our mouths are moving it is impossible to be still and think and remember. Our spiritual vision becomes clouded because we are too busy telling others of the small viewpoint of the day rather than remembering and pondering the grand vista of eternal perspective.

The mission president discovered why he was able to endure and continue to endure; because he remembered spiritual experiences of comfort and joy while he was in the midst of his trials.

Someone once said to never forget in the dark what God has told you in the light.

In recent years I have watched a good brother in the gospel fall away, let go of the rod, because he allowed himself to become swallowed by depression. As trials have come, he has spent his thoughts on how this could all be happening to him. Despite medical and spiritual help and lots of love and concern extended to him by family and friends, he has refused to give up self-pity. He has withdrawn from the Lord. He even blames God at times.

Thought replacement is not exclusive to psychology. Athletes use it to get ready for competition, even visualizing themselves winning. Soldiers use it before battle to overcome fear. Law enforcement officers use it to prepare to meet violent situations.

Thoughts, years of thoughts, bring us to where we find ourselves today. They started out as if they were flimsy cobwebs and have become unbreakable steel cables that either strengthen or shackle our ability to overcome trials and burdens and endure to the end.

"Therefore, sanctify yourselves that your minds become single to God, and the days will come that you shall see him. . . . Remember the great and last promise which I have made unto you; cast away your idle thoughts." (D&C 88:68–69.)

We are what we think and say. We also believe what we tell ourselves. My friend Joyce said over and over for years and years that she didn't have much self-confidence. Then, she received a new Church calling, one that would require much self-confidence. Worried and concerned, she turned to the Lord for help. Several days later, in conversation, she said out loud her familiar line, "I have no confidence." Almost as soon as those words left her lips, she heard a definite message of change. Into her mind came the thought, "That's your whole problem, stop saying that!" Today she is a changed woman.

Thinking is mostly talking to ourselves. It is what we think, conditioned by years of saying what we think, that makes us feel and believe ideas about ourselves and our lives. Eternal perspective is not simply thinking. Eternal perspective is "watching and looking."

"Do you *look forward* with an eye of faith, and view this mortal body raised in immortality, and this corruption raised in incorruption . . . ? I say unto you, *can you imagine* to yourselves that ye hear the voice of the Lord, saying unto you, in that day: Come unto me ye blessed, for behold, your works have been the works of righteousness upon the face of the earth?" (Alma 5:15–16; emphasis added.)

Insecure thoughts defeat us; secure thoughts inspire us.

Perhaps God has told us that there is something about us which is eternal, while at the same time placing us upon an earth where we all experience death, to remind *us how precious existence really is.* The fact that there is something, rather than nothing should cause us, at least for a few moments in the span of our lives, to be grateful that we, in fact, exist. We should remind ourselves that each person is important to God, and *we should be special to each other.* . . .

It is also possible that we have been told through the scriptures that we are eternal to keep us cognizant of how much we need each other. Whenever I get depressed or discouraged and, like Alma of old, want to cease to exist, I think of how much the existence of my wife, my children, and my fellow ward members mean to me. Then I become conscious once more, or at least hope once more, that there are some people who need me as much as I need them. (Kenneth W. Godfrey, "The History of Intelligence in Latter-day Saint Thought," in H. Donl Peterson and Charles D. Tate, Jr. eds., *The Pearl of Great Price: Revelations from God* [Provo: Religious Studies Center Brigham Young University, 1989], p. 233.)

As parents, we blunder and we succeed, only to fail again. We try, we try harder. We take parenting classes, we listen, we search, we pray, we repent, we try, we try harder. Yet, we face our weaknesses and inadequacies as parents not only every day, but also all day long.

If ever there were a day for remembering, this is that day. Our children are being bombarded by a great evil. If we as parents don't remember the spiritual experiences of comfort and count our blessings, we may become weak or faint-hearted in our efforts as parents. Then, who will fight for our children?

As we continue to battle Satan we must become good defense attorneys. He will ask us often, "Are you a good parent?" Our response is usually, "Yes." And then the battle begins:

Do your children argue?
Yes.

Do you raise your voice?
Yes.
Can they recite the thirteen articles of faith?
No.
Do they beg to say family prayers?
No.
Do they have clean rooms?
No.
Is family home evening always a bit of heaven?
No.
(and here comes the winner)
Do they get a hot dinner every night?
No.
How can you say you are a good parent then?
Because my children know I love the Savior, and I am teaching them to love him and to remember him. And because I love them and they know that too.

"And we talk of Christ, we rejoice in Christ, we preach of Christ, we prophesy of Christ, and we write according to our prophecies, that our children may know to what source they may look for a remission of their sins" (2 Nephi 25:26).

My son's high school English teacher asked the class what their idea of a perfect family was. The response was, the Cosbys, the Simpsons, and other television sitcom families. Chase's response was different. He said the idea of a perfect family was one that wasn't perfect at all, but a group of people who loved each other enough to help each other overcome problems, trials, and personal weaknesses.

One year ago we learned that our son had a life-threatening heart problem. He had been experiencing an extreme rapid heartbeat after exertion for the past two years. We had seen doctors, and he had been tested. The diagnosis was that he had a non-life-threatening ailment that we were told he would eventually outgrow. When a notable sports figure dropped dead because of a similar condition, our concern multiplied as we read about the symptoms this man had before he died. They seemed to be closely related to what our son was experiencing.

We decided to take him to a medical center that special-ized in the heart. The day before we went in for his testing, his father gave him a blessing in which he was promised he would be made whole. A tremendous witness was given to us during the blessing; a spiritual experience of comfort.

The next day we learned that his condition was an un-usual case of a rare type of ventricular tachycardia. We were told it was life threatening and inoperable. His heart was aging prematurely, and the best we could hope for was a pace-maker by the time he was twenty. We were told, with the rapid advances in technology, time would hopefully be on his side. His life would now be severely restricted. He could not partic-ipate in any sports or physical activity or go above altitudes of five thousand feet or below ten feet of water.

I stayed with him that night in the hospital while my hus-band flew back to Las Vegas. That evening we spoke by phone. He asked, "But what about the blessing, what did all that mean?" I could feel his sorrow. But the witness during the blessing had been real. We knew we had to exercise our faith. That blessing was from the Lord. We felt it. Maybe the procedure that would make Chase whole again hadn't been invented yet. We had to believe in that blessing.

Early the next morning one of the doctors came to the room. He said he had not been able to get Chase off his mind and that morning he had taken the case to the weekly break-fast meeting of all the heart surgeons. They had reviewed the data and the diagnosis. He told us that there was a new pro-cedure that was done only by three or four doctors in the en-tire country. They did not do it at their facility. The closest fa-cility that performed the procedure was at the University of California in San Francisco. The doctor told us it was the unanimous opinion of the group that morning that we should investigate this procedure and see if our son was a can-didate for it.

After a visit to the surgeon in San Francisco and still more tests, it was determined that Chase was indeed a candidate for the surgery. He was given a medication that would control the attacks, and a surgery date was scheduled four months from that time. We were told the procedure was only eighteen months old but the results were statistically excellent. There were no guarantees, but we were filled with new hope.

Within six weeks he began having breakthroughs in the medication. The arrhythmias were starting again. The medicine wasn't working. The surgery was immediately scheduled for the following Monday morning.

Chase, who had been seemingly nonchalant until this point, began to grow obviously nervous and afraid. No matter what we said, he seemed to grow more uncertain, more concerned about never returning home. Our ward held a special fast. That Sunday evening friends and family gathered in our home and knelt in prayer as the bishop prayed and asked the Lord to accept our offering.

We watched and felt an overpowering spirit of peace engulf the room, and especially Chase. With a trembling voice, he expressed his gratitude and love for their efforts in his behalf.

We boarded the plane that night, and he told me that no matter what happened he would always remember that sacred experience in our home. He said during the prayer he felt God's love for him, for the Saints, and for his family. He felt peace and he said he felt power, even power to overcome his fear and his great trial that lay in the path of his life. No matter what happened, he would never forget.

The surgery went well we were told, in fact, faster than they expected. That evening, in his hospital room, eight hours after surgery, he lay in his bed, foggy and struggling to recover from the anesthesia. He was sick and crying out in pain. The nurses kept trying in vain to make him comfortable. He was completely unaware of his surroundings and began to grow clammy and cold.

After standing by watching him struggle for several hours, he seemed to be getting worse. Unable to stand the uncertainty and panic for another moment, I quickly asked that a doctor immediately come examine him. Within minutes of the doctor's arrival, Chase was seized by another attack. Our hopes were dashed as we realized that the operation had not been successful at all. I felt paralyzed as I saw his blood pressure plummet on the monitor. As if in a nightmare, I heard the words *code blue* over the loudspeaker and watched, horrified, as doctors and nurses rushed into the room.

We were forced to stand outside in the hall, feeling utterly helpless, numbly watching the medical team work frantically to save his life. I wrapped spiritual arms around a rod of faith, witness, testimony, and prayers for the life of my son.

Standing in the hostility of that stark, white, lonely hall, my eyes frantically searched to find some part of him, some indication of life, the blush of his skin, but all I could find was his face white as a sheet, punctuating the chaos around his bed. If he was about to die, I wanted it to be in my arms and not under the cold, sterile hands of strangers. I was with him when he came into the world, I wanted to be with him and breathe with him his last breath if this was his time to leave.

All at once I was overcome with a new feeling. I felt as if that once lonely hallway was suddenly filled with friends and family, even my entire ward, comforting me and sustaining me with their prayers. I was encouraged and began again to remember. Many things that I needed to remember suddenly rushed into my mind: blessings, spiritual experiences, and whole verses of scriptures all brought me comfort. I was renewed as a peace began to wash over me and swell within me.

The Lord spared Chase's life. He spent the night in the intensive care unit. The next day the doctors expressed their desire to try again. They explained that they believed they had only stunned the area with the laser and had not destroyed the diseased cells. They knew where the cells were, even the exact spot. They believed that Chase had been so anesthetized that the area appeared clear when actually it had been only "stunned." They wanted to proceed again. However, there was one small catch. Chase would have to remain awake as long as possible in order for them to be absolutely certain they were successful. This had to be his choice.

He looked at us with a conviction in his eyes, and said, "I can do it. I remember the blessing, the fast, the prayers. I want to try again. I know Heavenly Father will help me."

The surgery took six and one-half hours. He was given no anesthetic. We were told they were successful in destroying all the diseased cells. When he was returned to the room one of the doctors personally pushed the gurney and helped the nurse gently get him into the bed. He expressed to us his admiration for Chase's character and told us that he had been deeply touched and affected by his courage. As the doctor and nurses left the room, finally leaving us alone together, Chase began to weep, unable to restrain the tears any longer. Then the words came; unable to restrain his emotions, he told us of the incredible spiritual experiences that he had during those grueling six and one-half hours of surgery.

They had given him a little anesthetic in the beginning to get the shunts into his arteries and up into his heart. For about the first twenty minutes he was okay. Then he began to feel the pain and the hideous sensation of the catheters in his heart. He heard the noises, listened to the dialogue of the medical team, felt the burning, smelled the nauseating antiseptic odors. Anxiety began to creep over him and he began to fall deeper and deeper into the clutches of fear. He wept and begged, "Please, please, you have to give me something." The doctor operating the catheter asked him to please hang on twenty or thirty more minutes so they could be more certain of success. Chase closed his eyes and began to pray silently, pleading for help. Suddenly, he remembered again the prayers, the blessing. As he lay thinking and meditating upon those words, he began to hear voices. He listened carefully and realized that he was hearing people praying for him. Calmness returned like a strange force, and he was able to go on for the next thirty minutes.

Then he began to feel more pain, and all his physical senses began again to be acutely aware of what was happening. He cried out for relief. Again, the doctor asked for more time. Just ten or fifteen minutes more they wanted. He prayed for strength, and again he heard people praying for him. He began to listen, this time concentrating on the voices. During the hours that followed this was how he overcame fear and panic. Just when he felt he could bear no more, the prayers would come to his mind. He began to hear and distinguish familiar voices. He said, "Mom, I heard you. This is what you said . . ." and he repeated to me the exact words and sentences I had prayed for him over the previous months and in the hours in the hospital. He said, "Dad, I heard you, and this is what you said. . . ." Again, he repeated Steve's exact words to the Lord. His uncle, aunt, and grandparents called, and he shared the same experience with them. That day of remembering will be with us all as the future unfolds more trials and tribulations. We can endure to the end. These memories and others like them, provide us with the ability to grip harder in the dark the rod we have seen only in the light.

Think back through your life. Do you remember the spiritual experiences that brought comfort and joy? These are the memories we must deliberately cultivate if we are to endure to the end and hold fast to the iron rod.

Many in this church sense the need to improve as a group as well as individually, otherwise we wouldn't be trying so hard to hold on to the rod. There are all levels of spirituality within the gospel net. All of us struggle with some form of pride and "memory loss." Some, perhaps, struggle to obey the Word of Wisdom. Some won't pay tithing. Others may not be diligent in Church callings. Some may not take counsel very well. Some may be unforgiving or jealous. Some may remember and dwell on only the darkness, some may be full of self-pity. Others may be high-minded and many, many more of us murmur. There are many ways to perish.

"And finally, I cannot tell you all the things whereby ye may commit sin; for there are divers ways and means, even so many that I cannot number them. But this much I can tell you, that if ye do not watch yourselves, and your thoughts, and your words, and your deeds, and observe the commandments of God, and continue in the faith of what ye have heard concerning the coming of our Lord, even unto the end of your lives, ye must perish. And now, O man, remember, and perish not." (Mosiah 4:29–30.)

The Lord understands that we may not always keep the commandments perfectly. He also knows that we may not always understand them. Nonetheless the Lord requires "the heart and a willing mind" (D&C 64:34), a heart full of gratitude and humility, a mind willing to remember the commandments and the Savior and be obedient (see D&C 46:9).

Watching the young women in the forest that night receive instructions at the top of the rope brought to my memory the words of Enoch that "many have believed and become the sons of God, and many have believed not, and have perished" (Moses 7:1).

We are laying the foundation of a great work. "Know ye not that ye are the temple of God?" (1 Corinthians 3:16.)

There can be no victory if there is no battle. If we can, through more gratitude, cultivate more memory, we can become more patient, more humble, more meek, more like the Savior.

And then, if we choose to remember the goodness of the Lord in our lives in the dark abyss of some sore trial, we can recall the words, perhaps said long, long ago: "Now, *remember,* no matter what happens, never, never let go of the rod."

2

REMEMBER, THE WORTH OF SOULS IS GREAT

*Remember the worth of souls
is great in the sight of God.
—D&C 18:10*

*E*ven though we aren't fully worthy, we are full of worth.

Wouldn't it be wonderful if we could remember the night of the Savior's birth; recalling the day we may have bid him farewell as he left our home in the preexistence? Perhaps we stood on the edge of the eternities and witnessed firsthand the marvelous events of that holy night. Maybe even some of us sang in those heavenly choirs heard by the shepherds.

Consider the possibility of remembering another night in the Savior's life, the night in Gethsemane. Do you think we may have been praying that he would be comforted and strengthened on this the night of all nights? From this garden setting came the proof that the worth of souls is great. Perhaps we prayed that night to never forget it. What would it do for us to be able to remember even the journey to the cross and the remarkable resurrection that bore witness of immortality and the possibility of eternal life?

Would these kind of memories dispel our tendencies to question our worth, especially when we try to balance our worth against our weakness? Do we forget that weaknesses are not sins? We are given weaknesses so that we will be humble.

"I give unto men weakness that they may be humble" (Ether 12:27).

We need this humility to cultivate memory, to remember to turn to our God for help. We need to remember him in order to cultivate greater faith in ourselves and to remember the great sacrifice of the Savior in order to strengthen that faith in God in others and in ourselves.

I'm not sure the prospects of this earth life were so joyful. The reality of a world of pain and sorrow had to have been explained to us. To me, the fact that I would not be able to remember surely was a very chilling thought. But we knew we had to come. To be like Father and Mother in Heaven it was necessary to leave them and develop fully here; even though it must have looked grim, we had to go. We believed it would be for our own good. We must have believed we could hold to the rod.

Maybe we were more able and ready to go because we did know our worth and feel God's love for us.

So we came, and here we are. This is definitely *the world.* Some of us are now crossing deserts of spiritual dryness, feeling desolation in climbing mountains of doubt, swimming oceans of turbulent trials, and wandering on plains of sorrow, or, like my young sisters at girls' camp, stumbling through forests of darkness.

What treasure would you give to remember the worth you felt in the presence of heavenly parents? What would you pay to know on dark days how those heavenly parents are reaching across deserts, mountains, oceans, and forests, anxious to hold us close and bring us safely home?

The older I grow, the longer I live, as naive and simple as this may seem to say, the more I see how much God loves us and loves us unconditionally. This understanding has deepened not in spite of my trials in life, but because of them. Somehow, my memory has been enlarged because of difficulties and sorrows. I know he really, truly loves us.

He loves us because we are his children, he begat us. Just as a mortal father loves his child, flesh of his flesh, bone of his bone, Heavenly Father loves instinctively and transcendently.

The worth of souls is great because we are of infinite worth. We are the children of our heavenly parents and they number each one of us. I know we can have a better memory of this as we observe the unconditional love of little children for mankind.

When our youngest child was two or three, my husband, Steve, took her with him to a thrift store that always carried old magazines and postcards. He placed her in the shopping cart, next to his side, as he thumbed through a stack of old magazines, looking for a specific issue. Intrigued and lost in thought, he was only slightly aware of her jabbering until he was jarred into reality as he realized she was trying to climb out of the cart.

With his attention now turned away from his cache of antiques, he began to focus on the object of her effort to be free.

She was pointing and talking in her toddler's jabber to a young man about ten feet away, an employee of the thrift store. Steve turned his full attention to Paige's chatter and tried to figure out what she wanted from this young man.

He immediately saw that this man had been in some kind of serious accident, probably a fire or burn accident. His legs were dragging limply behind him, an arm was severely burned and shriveled. His face and head had been so disfigured that the right side of his chin seemed to have melted into his neck. An ear, an eye, and most of his nose were gone. Only a few absurd tufts of hair remained impossibly among the screaming mass of bright red scar tissue. He was gruesome in appearance.

At first, Steve feared Paige's curiosity, concerned that she might offend the man. Then he soon realized it wasn't curiosity at all, she was trying to reach out to the man to give him a hug! He had been shaking his head at her trying to discourage her when finally he looked up at Steve as if to say, "What do I do?" Steve smiled and simply nodded his head in approval. The young man slowly shuffled closer to her as she reached out to hug him. Reverently, he just slightly touched her hand with his whole one. She grabbed his arm and hugged him unabashedly. Then she looked up at him, smiling and giggling like only a toddler can do, and said, "I wuv you!" Overcome with emotion, he quickly turned and walked away, brushing tears from his cheek.

After paying for his purchases, Steve noticed him standing near the front doors. He approached Steve and placed in his hand an old, very worn, green stuffed animal. His voice trembling with choking emotion he said, "Please, give this to her, and tell her someday what she meant to me."

Have you ever felt alone and lonely and of little value, probably much like that young man felt most of the time? Wouldn't it be of such comfort to us if we could remember that love that God has for us and remember how much we are worth and that he loves us just because we are his?

What happens if we fail to grasp our sense of divine worth?

We become self-conscious, insincere, self-absorbed, negative, judgmental, critical, languishing in mediocrity. We look for self-esteem through self-serving.

Any road to self-esteem is a false road unless every man "esteem his brother as himself" (D&C 38:25).

A successful businessman who depends on first impressions told me that he read a study that concluded people form a permanent impression of someone in the first four minutes of meeting them. It is possible to change that opinion, but it takes a long time and is usually not easily changed.

This made me think about all the times I am in such a hurry. I probably give the impression that I am unconcerned with others a lot of the time. A man that recently moved into our ward told my husband that he thought I was such a quiet person. Steve thought that was funny and told him he just didn't know me very well! Because he had been in the ward only a short time I supposed that he had me mixed up with someone else and didn't really know who Steve's wife was. Steve reassured me this man knew which woman he was describing.

I wondered what he had seen of me that made him think I was a very quiet person.

Suppose two people from your family were sent back for four minutes to report on the relationship of Nephi and Laman and Lemuel. One went back for four minutes during the time they were working together on building the ship. The other went back during the ocean crossing when Nephi was tied to the ship.

In four minutes permanent impressions would be formed. One person would report of a cohesive brotherhood, supporting one another and working together. The other report would be of jealousy, pride, and disobedience.

We cannot judge one another. We cannot let our opinions be formed in four minutes, four months, or four years. This is a gospel where the worth of souls is great. We are not fully worthy but we are full of worth. We will respect others' worth as we respect our own. We will reaffirm our children's worth as we reaffirm our own. We cannot overemphasize the worth of a soul to retain and reclaim our children.

He loves us because we chose to be like him. This is the part we probably fail to remember the most. This is a part worth pondering. We did not come to this earth without making a definite decision. We had a choice. The choice was not whether or not we wanted agency. Agency is an eternal law. We had a choice in the preexistence, we have choices here. The choice was whether or not we wanted to become like our heavenly parents. Did we want a body of flesh and bones like them? Did we want to become exalted like them? Did we want to have the kind of life they have—eternal life? Did we want immortality? Did we want to do it according to the plan of salvation? We had a choice. Perhaps in those choices were many levels of commitment.

That level of commitment, however, has nothing to do with God's love for us. Everyone who is born on the earth chose to be like him, to have a body of flesh and bones, to partake of his existence. There were a third who did not choose that.

He loves us because we loved the Savior and his plan. The prospects of a life away from God with absolutely no memory of our life before must have been somewhat unsettling. Undoubtedly there were thousands of questions of concern, perhaps fear. Even as the plan of salvation was presented I cannot imagine us saying, "Oh, a life of trial, sorrow, pain? How wonderful!" The idea of no remembrance of "former friends and birth" must have caused some unrest.

We loved the Savior and his plan enough to willingly submit, even with a shout of joy. We were witnesses of the Savior's submission to the Father's will, "Here am I, send me" (Abraham 3:27). We saw his willingness to sacrifice himself for our redemption. We saw the joy he brought to the Father. God loves us for our acceptance of the Savior, for our desire to be submissive.

He loves us because we qualified ourselves to come to earth. When we chose the Savior and his plan it was not the end of our qualification. As the gospel teaches the principle of *works,* can we ponder that there were *works* before we came here as well?

Perhaps in a preexistence schooling we chose or qualified ourselves to be born into particular places at particular times for particular reasons. Maybe spiritual gifts and talents were given or earned so that in our individual circumstances on earth, all, including ourselves, "may be profited thereby" (D&C 46:12).

He loves us because he knows us. He knows things about us we don't know, things we can't remember. He sees our uniqueness and potential for greatness. He knows us better than we know ourselves.

There is a story about a woman who joined an elite book club. At one social she met a man who was interested in discussing a current best-selling novel. The woman told him she didn't like the book and couldn't get past the third chapter.

After more discussion, he invited her for dinner. Soon they began dating, and a wonderful friendship developed. Some months later he revealed to her that he was an author who wrote under an assumed name. When he revealed the pen name, she was astonished to find that he was the author of the book she had told him she didn't like! They had a good laugh, but she now had a new desire to read the book. Why? Because now she really knew the author.

This time she was fascinated. She couldn't put the book down. She saw the deeper concepts in the characters' dialogue. She thoroughly enjoyed every word.

What had changed? She had grown to know the author. She saw in his writing much more now because she now knew much more about him.

So, God loves us because he knows us. He knows us better than we know ourselves. He sees things in us we don't even see in ourselves.

He loves us because we look like him. I remember those unforgettable moments of first seeing my own children. Every time, I was in awe of their perfect little bodies, miniature adults. I was awed by the immediate resemblances I saw connecting them to generations of progenitors.

We are created in his image! We look like him. But, also, he sees a lot of himself in us. And he sees we are capable of becoming like him.

In Keeneland, Kentucky, a yearling sold for ten million dollars. This horse had never run a race. Why would the price be so high for a horse yet unproven?

It is because the owners were aware of the horse's potential. The yearling's bloodline was of champions. The horse had descended from a heritage of great worth. The owners knew things about this horse that the horse had not yet proven or shown. How much more clearly can we see our worth when we remember God is our father?

He loves us because he is proud of us. We are his children in whom he is well pleased. He knows coming to earth shows our desire to do the right thing. He realizes that it was hard for us to come, knowing we would be away from him. He sees us weathering great trials and tribulation—suffering, but not giving up on him. He is so proud of us.

Recently, one of our children wanted to go on a wilderness survival experience in order to have the opportunity to deepen his understanding of his own potential.

He went during the summer months to a desert area where water was scarce and the temperatures soared to over 115 degrees Fahrenheit.

On one occasion his perception of how our Father in Heaven is proud of us was enlarged as he saw a fellow student struggle and then succeed.

They had been walking and hiking for days under the searing desert sun. There was one boy who had been in their group only a few days. He was overweight, but heavier still was his negative attitude.

After struggling for a few hours, this boy threw his backpack down and refused to go on. This meant the entire group was compelled to come to a standstill. The boys became angry and frustrated. They had put up with him for long enough. Now they all were parched, thirsty and exhausted, and impatient. They needed to get to their final destination that day. There was no water. The truck would be there with water. They needed to rest. They needed to succeed that day.

The group began to chastise him. Hostile words were flung like weapons. The frustration mounted. My son was equally upset with him. But, no amount of pleading, coaxing, or harassment would move him; the boy refused to budge.

Suddenly my son looked at him from a new perspective, and a feeling of love swept over him. He began to see the effort that it had taken for this troubled boy to have even come this far. He had been really trying to keep up with the group. He had pushed himself beyond the limits of anything he had ever attempted before. But, he was full of weakness; that weakness had overcome him, and he had become discouraged.

Amid the murmuring, my son walked over, picked up the boy's pack and said, "Come on, you can make it, because I'm going to carry your pack." The group grew silent, everyone knew how hard it was just to carry your own pack, not to mention two of them, over rough terrain in broiling, unbearable heat. Another boy stepped forward through the crowd and said to my son, "And when you're tired, I'll carry it the rest of the way."

There was a feeling of love that continued for the rest of the weeks they were together. They strengthened one another. They truly were proud, well pleased, with one another.

Our Father looks down from his heavenly throne upon our efforts, observing with solicitude even those efforts in which he has helped us carry our burdens, and he loves us because he is well pleased with those efforts.

He loves us because he is perfect. He is perfect, so his love is perfect. What is perfect love?

"And charity suffereth long, and is kind, and envieth not, and is not puffed up, seeketh not her own, is not easily provoked, thinketh no evil, and rejoiceth not in iniquity but rejoiceth in the truth, beareth all things, believeth all things, hopeth all things, endureth all things" (Moroni 7:45).

This kind of love sounds like it is the kind of love that hurts. It is easy to love people who are lovable. It is painful to love those who are bitter, spiteful, lazy, rebellious, prideful, revengeful, dirty, or unclean. It is especially painful to love those who reject our love.

Yet God loves us perfectly, charitably, because he is a perfect God.

He loves us because he sacrificed for us. "For God so loved the world, that he gave his only begotten Son" (John 3:16).

My first pregnancy was a physical hardship. It was like the nine-month flu. It was difficult to keep food down. I retained fluid so much that I could wear only stretch slippers on my feet and my rings had to be cut off. During the last weeks I couldn't sleep, and breathing became an effort.

My little grandmother, Mamagrande, came to visit my father a few weeks before the baby was due. I complained to her extensively, a detailed description of all the things I didn't like about being pregnant. She listened patiently and intently until I was completely finished. Then she taught me an eternal principle.

Without lifting her gaze from her careworn hands she said in her charming, broken English, "Yes, but you are sacrificing so you will love your child."

As the Savior went into Gethsemane and the hours of the Atonement began to unfold, it was much worse than even he had expected. He "began to be sore amazed, and to be very heavy" (Mark 14:33). He pleaded at one point during those agonizing hours that "if it were possible, the hour might pass from him" (Mark 14:35). The Savior then reaffirmed that he would do his Father's will, but the reality of the gruesome agony caused even this perfect Son to beg for an end to it. He called upon his Father, knowing God had the power to do anything—all things—and pleaded, "Father, all things are possible unto thee; take away this cup from me" (Mark 14:36).

What father's heart would not be wrenched with longing to see his son in some excruciating pain that he would not do anything in his power to end it? Here was God the Father, all knowing, all powerful. Here was his perfect, obedient, loving Son, asking, if it were possible, for help.

Both Christ and God the Father knew it was possible and that the power was there to end it. What suffering and sacrifice the Father must have gone through in order to restrain himself during those dreadful hours! He sacrificed for us, because he loves us so much.

He loves us because he loves his work and his glory. What person doesn't love his accomplishments, the workmanship of his own hands, his glories? God loves his work, which is to bring to pass our immortality and eternal life (see Moses 1:39).

We get the meaning of our real worth all entangled in our performance. If that isn't bad enough, we then measure our performance against everyone else's. We then become vulnerable to Satan's diabolical suggestions that everyone in the Church has their life in order but us.

It is unfortunate that our worth has been described with this reasoning. But no earthly performance will be noted except our effort to endure our trials. Our *real* worth is the center of all the Savior's efforts to prepare, instruct, and implement the plan of salvation and exaltation in our lives. Our real worth is the reason he paid the price he did. And he paid it because he believed many would follow him. There is an overshadowing belief among many that only a few are going to make it to the celestial kingdom. I've even heard that preached a time or two in my lifetime. Someone once even suggested the parable of the ten virgins meant half would make it, half wouldn't. Those kinds of numbers and statistics don't inspire me much. But what does inspire me is a much more encouraging account of how many will make it.

> After this I beheld, and, lo, a great multitude, which no man could number, of all nations, and kindreds, and people, and tongues, stood before the throne, and before the Lamb, clothed with white robes, and palms in their hands; . . .
>
> And one of the elders answered, saying unto me, What are these which are arrayed in white robes? and whence came they?
>
> And I said unto him, Sir, thou knowest. And he said to me, These are they which came out of great tribulation, and have washed their robes, and made them white in the blood of the Lamb.

Therefore are they before the throne of God, and serve him day and night in his temple: and he that sitteth on the throne shall dwell among them.

They shall hunger no more, neither thirst any more; neither shall the sun light on them, nor any heat. (Revelation 7:9, 13–16.)

How many? "A great multitude, which no man could number."

A friend of mine who works with statistics for a living told me that it is possible for a man to be able to number millions, but it would nearly be impossible for a man to be able to number billions.

As author Stephen E. Robinson has explained, we have to not only believe in Christ, but we have to believe him when he says he is our Savior and our worth is great to him. He wants us to come home, he wants us back. He is counting his sheep, and he is rescuing the ones who have strayed. This is the gospel of the Shepherd, whose watchful eye and hand are over all his little lambs; all are of great value to him, even those lambs that are greatly blemished—mottled, spotted, or black with sin.

He has provided a way for us to always return to the flock. And if we are slow in returning, he is about his "work" in saving us, helping us hold fast to the rod.

I have a very good friend who has been a wayward lamb for much of her life. She has forsaken the past and in recent years has been a faithful follower, one of "the believers." But she had been plagued with the memory of her many mistakes. She had feelings of worthlessness as she worked along the side of those whom she perceived had led more honorable lives. She could not remove the memory of her sins. She had repented, she had been forgiven, why couldn't she forget? She felt weighed down by her memories, until she read one night these words:

And it came to pass that I was thus racked with torment, while I was harrowed up by the memory of my many sins, behold, I remembered also to have heard my father prophesy unto the people concerning the coming of one Jesus Christ, a Son of God, to atone for the sins of the world.

Now, as my mind caught hold upon this thought, I cried within my heart: O Jesus, thou Son of God, have mercy on me, who am in the gall of bitterness, and am encircled about by the everlasting chains of death.

And now, behold, when I thought this, I could remember my pains no more; yea, I was harrowed up by the memory of my sins no more.

And oh, what joy, and what marvelous light I did behold; yea, my soul was filled with joy as exceeding as was my pain! (Alma 36:17–20.)

She probably would always remember some of her sins, but she finally came to the understanding that she really had been forgiven, because even though she could remember the sins, she was unable to remember the pains of those sins. What she could remember was the sweetness of the spirit and the joy of being able to take the sacrament. The personal vision of her own worth to God was renewed.

Perhaps Satan's greatest weapon against a people who are really trying to be a part of something better is to attack their feelings of self-worth. It can be an overwhelming experience to be crushed under his power of discouragement. His discouraging suggestions can also tempt us into hopelessness.

I was impressed by Sister Chieko Okazaki's talk at the 1994 General Relief Society meeting in which she counseled us to learn by study and by faith. She held in her hands two wooden oars, the kind used to row a boat. On one was written the word faith, the other the word study. She described how if we were to row with only one oar we would go only in circles. We need both oars to row to our destination. In other words, both learning by study and learning by faith are required to hold to the rod. (See "Rowing Your Boat," *Ensign,* November 1994, pp. 92–94.)

If we concentrate solely on one method of learning, we will become unbalanced. It is unbalance that causes us to wobble and waver, even fall. The risk in that is that we can fall hard enough and far away enough as to lose our grip on the rod.

Perhaps you have experienced learning by study alone. The result is often a "mind hardened in pride" (Daniel 5:20) and the temptation to love one's own opinion too much. Hardened minds are not soft enough to recognize and absorb spiritual witnesses. Memory is difficult to release when it is held captive in steel cells of prideful opinion. Study brings us self-reliance. But self-reliance without faith brings pride.

I spoke briefly with a sister who has long let go of the rod. Her daughters are now old enough to participate in the Young Women program and remain unbaptized. She is successful in her talents and is a lovely and amiable person. She told me, however, that things didn't work out for her in the Church and that her own children would have to find out for themselves what they wanted of religion in their lives. Her other chosen paths were the result of learning by study alone. She told me that when her girls were young she began to study divergent philosophical views and found life to be so much more rewarding than the narrow perspective the gospel gives.

Without attempting to judge this good woman, may I add that if learning by faith had been an equal part of the curriculum then perhaps *eternal perspective* would have been revealed.

Likewise, we have all seen what happens when we neglect learning by study and try to learn by faith alone. Without a foundation of skills and/or knowledge, faith alone will not produce self-reliance. When problems arise, if we do not have skills or knowledge, faith alone will not give us enough confidence to hold fast to the rod.

There is a sister that believed all her life that she had only to grow up, get married, have children, and go to church to be happy. She did just that. There was no effort extended, very little anyway, to read or study or prepare herself for any of life's unexpected pitfalls. As she reached maturity, and the years began to pass more rapidly, she began to notice the talents and skills of fellow sisters around her. She felt diminished by the success of others. She truly believed it was too late. She often made the statement, "I have no talents." Her home was untidy, her appearance, though immaculate, was dowdy, and her confidence was weak. She never participated in open discussions and never prayed in public.

Life's small pitfalls became cavernous depths as she slipped deeper and deeper into withdrawal until she was completely inactive. Today it is difficult to discuss the gospel with her. She is a wonderful woman and she does have a testimony but is unable to cope with the crisis after crisis that have come into her life.

She was unprepared and now faces financial, emotional, and physical hardships. Even her faith, which once sustained her, now wavers uncontrollably.

These two examples are both cases of deception. We are deceived not only by Satan and those who are under his influence, but we are also deceived by false precepts and by our own weaknesses. So that we will not be deceived, and so that we will not perish, we have been counseled by the Savior to seek spiritual gifts, "always remembering for what they are given" (D&C 46:8).

Seeking spiritual gifts aids us in learning by both study and faith because as we seek the gifts, the Holy Ghost will inspire us in all things we need in order to be successful in maintaining that balance.

Some years ago I was asked to head an interior design project that was really over my head. It was a multimillion-dollar project that would require painstaking and meticulously detailed planning of the interior architecture and furnishings. The project, quite frankly, terrified me, and I was tempted to decline it.

An unceasing mental battle of *Can I? Can't I?* weighed on my thoughts for weeks. Little by little I sorted through the facts. It was beyond my present skill level. There were other designers more qualified. This project would bring more projects of the same caliber. What if I failed miserably? But didn't nineteen years in the profession count for something? Had not I achieved some higher level of expertise? Throughout these embattled questions came a clear, precise thought. Make a decision and then take it to the Lord. I made the decision to take the risk, accept the job, and ask the Lord for a confirmation. When it was received I then asked for help to remember all the good things I had ever seen that would be of use to me in this project. I asked also for gifts of inspiration, enlightenment, and illumination in my research and study and to be led by the Spirit in all decisions.

The project lasted four years. I spent countless hours researching in books and with experts in various fields of design. I assembled together a team of technicians and contractors that actually executed the difficult design ideas. The installation of just the interior finishes and details took a full year.

When it was finished, it was a work of art.

I attribute the entire success to learning both by study and by faith through spiritual gifts. I give all the credit to the Lord. He helped me do something I didn't know I could do. He helped me reach beyond my grasp and strengthen my self-reliance.

Spiritual gifts strengthen our personal grip upon the iron rod. They do this by (1) shielding us from the power of Satan, (2) giving us feelings of worth and joy, (3) compensating for our inadequacies, (4) repairing our imperfections and helping us to see our potential, (5) leading us to Christ, and (6) inspiring us to endure to the end, holding fast to the iron rod.

It is through remembrance that we will continue to seek spiritual gifts by both study and faith. Without remembering we will be "ever learning, and never able to come to the knowledge of the truth" (2 Timothy 3:7).

1. Spiritual gifts shield us from the power of Satan.

During my calling as the Laurel class adviser I had the opportunity to become very close to many of the girls in that class. One of these girls was dating a very popular, handsome boy who often accompanied her to youth activities, though he was not a member.

One particular Sunday morning I had prepared a lesson on developing talents. As soon as we entered the Young Women's meeting room for opening exercises I felt impressed to change the lesson to one on morality and chastity. I insisted to myself that was ridiculous, I wasn't prepared. But the feeling grew stronger. Suddenly, I couldn't remember what I had prepared!

By the time we separated for classes, I had managed to collect a few thoughts and began to present them to these young sisters of mine. The Spirit was very strong, words came easily, I could feel the Lord reaching out to his precious daughters, trying to impress upon them the importance of these messages. Then I told them of my husband's counsel to our own daughters. He has always told them there are two kinds of men in the world and only two kinds: the Protectors and the Seducers. The Seducers will seek to compromise a woman at any level. They think only of themselves and their own personal sensual gratification. They do not honor the tenderness of women. But the Protectors are not unlike Joseph who was sold into Egypt. They are trustworthy. They honor womanhood. They are loyal to God and the commandments. They are men of great integrity. They put the feelings of others first.

That very evening I received a midnight visitor. It was this girl who had been dating Mr. Wonderful. She poured out her heart to me. He was a good person, very kind and thoughtful. He had professed his love for her, and he had wanted intimacy. He was persuasive, and the feelings she had for him were powerful.

She wept as she described how some of the very words I used that very morning were complete sentences from her patriarchal blessing. She had felt the power and influence of a loving God reaching out to her with a voice of warning. She had decided with conviction, but not without a little sadness, to break off her romantic relationship with this boy.

I watched this young woman go forward with a new sense of her self-worth, more confident than she has ever been before. That day she picked up the shield of her spiritual gifts and defended her soul against the devil. She was then and is now a righteous woman and a mighty instrument in the hands of the Lord. Her spiritual gifts of humility shielded her from the power of Satan. Do you think she has grown in feelings of personal worth?

We have a friend, a medical doctor in our community, a faithful Church member who has held responsible Church positions. He related to us his response to a growing appeal from a group of Church members soliciting others not to pay their income tax. He had been intrigued by the discussion of how it was possible to avoid this government regulation. His taxes were, because of his income, always very high and always very complicated. He went with great curiosity to the meeting. He listened as others told of how it was done and of how illegal the tax is and how wrong and corrupt our government is. The arguments were convincing and well delivered. He sat there and listened carefully and paid attention to the feelings of his heart.

As he got up to leave, he remembered the twelfth article of faith: "We believe in being subject to kings, presidents, rulers, and magistrates, in obeying, honoring, and sustaining the law."

It didn't matter to him whether those individuals spoke some truth. The Spirit testified to him of the Lord's disapproval and reaffirmed to him his responsibility to obey, honor, and sustain the law. It became clear to him that if we don't like the laws we can be instruments to change them, but not in this way. His spiritual gift of integrity shielded him from the power of Satan.

Much time has passed since that meeting, and some of those who were present and became a part of that movement are no longer members of the Church. Satan carefully leads us to hell (see 2 Nephi 28:21).

Do you think this man feels a greater confidence in the presence of the Lord? I think so.

Another friend of ours, a veil worker, related to us the story of how the spiritual gift of obedience shielded one man from the power of Satan.

Two men were called at approximately the same time to be veil workers, both men had full beards, but that was the extent of the similarity between them. One man was in good health; very active in life and had a prosperous business. The other man was poor in health; restricted from a lot of physical activity and struggling financially.

The temple president required that all veil workers be clean shaven. When these two men learned of this, the healthy man protested. He asked why God would care about such a thing. The Savior had a beard, some former latter-day prophets had beards. The man in poor health said nothing and returned to the temple clean shaven.

Within a few weeks the brother who refused to shave quit coming. The other brother continued to serve. He became healthier; in fact, he is today in excellent health. He prospered financially. The other man suffered financially and today he is in poor health. He is no longer active in the Church.

Which man has grown in his feelings of personal worth from a spiritual gift of humility?

2. Spiritual gifts give us feelings of worth and joy.

All my life in the Church I have heard some say how hard it is to live the gospel; that keeping the commandments is difficult. It is true that keeping all the commandments, all of the time, is not only difficult, it is impossible for us in the condition in which we now live. We live in a telestial world with telestial bodies, surrounded by opposition. The plan was to provide for us a Savior because we could not make it alone.

But I've lived long enough now to know that it is far more difficult to not try to keep the commandments! Breaking the laws of God leads only to broken hearts. Our lives run more smoothly, and we are more effective in dealing with our trials when we have the Lord on our side. If we will just be obedient, even if we aren't perfect in all things all the time, we will be blessed with the gift of meekness. When we are meek, we are then able to have the spirit and to cultivate all other spiritual gifts that will give us the power to be victorious.

I know of no other way that true feelings of worth come, except through the spiritual gift of meekness. I have tried many other routes to self-esteem, and sometimes they have dead-ended in self-worship. The peace and love and inner worth has come to me only through submission.

Consider Ammon. Fourteen years he diligently labored with his brethren to preach to the Lamanites. He used his spiritual gifts throughout his ministry, and they sustained him and blessed his own life as well as thousands of others. He spoke a powerful sermon on self-esteem:

> How great reason have we to rejoice; for could we have supposed when we started from the land of Zarahemla that God would have granted unto us such great blessings? . . .
>
> . . . For our brethren, the Lamanites, were in darkness, yea, even in the darkest abyss, but behold, how many of them are brought to behold the marvelous light of God! And this is the blessing which hath been bestowed upon us, that we have been made instruments in the hands of God to bring about this great work.
>
> Behold, thousands of them do rejoice, and have been brought into the fold of God. . . .
>
> For if we had not come up out of the land of Zarahemla, these our dearly beloved brethren, who have so dearly beloved

us, would still have been racked with hatred against us, yea, and they would also have been strangers to God.

And it came to pass that when Ammon had said these words, his brother Aaron rebuked him, saying: Ammon, I fear that thy joy doth carry thee away unto boasting.

But Ammon said unto him: I do not boast in my own strength, nor in my own wisdom; but behold, my joy is full, yea, my heart is brim with joy, and I will rejoice in my God.

Yea, I know that I am nothing; as to my strength I am weak; therefore I will not boast of myself, but I will boast of my God, for in his strength I can do all things; yea, behold, many mighty miracles we have wrought in this land, for which we will praise his name forever. (Alma 26:1–4, 9–12.)

He was meek, but full of strength, acknowledging that his great strength and ability came from God. Meekness is strength turned tender, strength turned over to the Lord. The spiritual gift of meekness cultivates self-worth.

The spiritual gift of charity is also worth pondering. How often have we heard the statement that you cannot love others until you love yourself.

My experience has been different than that, in fact, the exact opposite. It has been in the giving away of love to others that love for self has come.

Throughout my life I have watched others grow in confidence and self-worth as they used their spiritual gifts to benefit the kingdom of God. An inner knowledge of divine nature is personally cultivated as we develop and use spiritual gifts, especially as we use those gifts to build and raise others.

As a Young Women president, I was fully aware of the lack of confidence and worth with which youth often struggle. If the rise from adolescence to adulthood is without an understanding of how to overcome these feelings, the struggle can go on for years. Often, our youth believe that accomplishments equal worth. If they don't gain a better perspective, they go on into adulthood still measuring their worth against the performance of themselves versus others.

We had our young women make simple construction paper mobiles one evening, and then we proceeded to a local hospital's children's ward to deliver them. Upon our arrival we discovered that it was a children's trauma center we were about to visit. We explained to the girls that there might be some things that would be difficult to see. I don't think any of us were prepared for what happened.

Upon arriving on the floor the girls disappeared into the rooms and began to hang the mobiles and talk to the children. It was very apparent that most of the children had been abused and were recovering from severe beatings.

One little boy, about six years old, was frightened when several girls entered his room. He wouldn't talk, he wouldn't look at the mobile. He wouldn't respond except to fix his gaze on them as if afraid to let them out of his sight. The girls felt awkward. They stood silently for a few moments, uncertain of what to say. Then one had the idea to sing and began to lead out with the tender melody of "I Am a Child of God." A sweet spirit entered the room. They sang two or three more songs. Their soft, feminine voices attracted others, and more girls filled the room. I felt as if angels had come and caught my breath, feeling that these girls had created a little pocket of heaven in that solitary hospital room. I looked at the child, who still had not uttered a word, and saw tears coming down his cheeks. Then he turned over, closed his eyes, subdued by the melody of the Spirit, and fell asleep.

Many of the young women were also weeping, touched by the spirit of compassion and love. A new sense of confidence had come over them. They went from room to room with their angel voices, intoning song after song like silvery bells giving comfort and love to the little ones. I saw their hearts become tender, and I saw these girls who usually look in every mirror they pass, forget themselves and grow that night in confidence.

My own teenage daughter was among this group, and I saw her feelings and understanding of the worth of others deepen as she too partook of the spirit of charity that evening.

Our accomplishments of talent, career, education, or any other worldly pursuit will never produce feelings of worth or love for ourselves like loving others will.

I know about this because I tried it the other way. It doesn't work. It is complete emptiness. Yes, in the beginning, the moments of glory or success or praise are exhilarating. But oh they are so short-lived! So temporary! You must continually seek those moments to keep up the feelings of glory, for they are fleeting and pass swiftly.

How unlike the eternal feelings of worth that when cultivated and nurtured are constant as long as we love others and serve others and stretch to see their worth. As we see the worth of others through love and service we look in a mirror and begin to see our own worth.

3. Spiritual gifts compensate for our inadequacies.

Elder Neal A. Maxwell said: "God does not begin by asking about our ability, but only about our availability, and if we then prove our dependability, he will increase our capability!" (*The Neal A. Maxwell Quote Book,* ed. Cory H. Maxwell [Salt Lake City: Bookcraft, 1997], p. 1.)

I met a woman in Mississippi some years ago who, after some vacillation, eventually exercised her gift of dependability and deepened her feelings of worth.

She approached me as I entered the chapel just moments before I was to speak. She wanted to visit briefly about something that was deeply troubling her. She had been the Young Women president in her ward for several years. She had been in the Young Women program for over eleven years. She felt comfortable there. She felt that she could serve best with the younger sisters of the Church. The older sisters scared her. She wasn't comfortable teaching them. The dilemma was that the bishop had recently released her as Young Women president and had asked her to be a Relief Society teacher. She had declined. Now she felt troubled. She wanted to serve, but this was too big a burden. She was practically immobilized by fear.

She asked me how she could convince the bishop to put her back in the Young Women program. My response was that I didn't know how. But I did know something else—the Lord knew things about her that she didn't. He knows our potential and what we can accomplish. He places at the head of a ward or branch a good and just man whom he can inspire to put us in callings that will help us see our potential.

I told her that if she accepted the call, she would probably find talents she never knew she had. We did not speak again that day. When the conference was over I left for home.

About a year or so later a letter came from Mississippi. It was from this sister, telling me of how she had chosen to accept the call after all. She described her struggle at first and then wrote of the great growth she experienced. But this was only part of the purpose of her letter. She was writing to inform me she had just been set apart that day as the ward Relief Society president!

Her spiritual gift of dependability helped her compensate for her inadequacies.

4. Spiritual gifts repair our imperfections and help us see our potential.

Recently I watched a television documentary on the life of Wilma Rudolph, the great American athlete who had been afflicted with polio as a child. Through determination and will she overcame her handicap and won three gold medals in the 1960 Olympics in the 100-, 200-, and 400-meter relays, breaking the world record for the 200 meter. She almost *overcompensated*.

This brings to mind the great scripture in Ether: "And if men come unto me I will show unto them their weakness. I give unto men weakness that they may be humble; and my grace is sufficient for all men that humble themselves before me; for if they humble themselves before me, and have faith in me, then will I make weak things become strong unto them" (Ether 12:27).

Are we given weaknesses in the very places we are expected to excel? Through, first, the spiritual gift of humility we come to the Lord. He then can bless us with other gifts we need in order to turn weakness into strength.

Enoch asked if the Lord was sure he had the right man for the work. "And when Enoch had heard these words, he bowed himself to the earth, before the Lord, and spake before the Lord, saying: Why is it that I have found favor in thy sight, and am but a lad, and all the people hate me; for I am slow of speech; wherefore am I thy servant?" (Moses 6:31.)

The Lord told Enoch that if he would be obedient, he would be given spiritual gifts, and his imperfections would be repaired. "Open thy mouth, and it shall be filled, and I will give thee utterance" (Moses 6:32).

This young Enoch was probably taunted by his peers with a brutality not unlike the cruelty children lash out with against one another today. But spiritual gifts likely helped Enoch overcome his fear, feel a great sense of his own worth, and witness victory over his own imperfection. "And as Enoch spake forth the words of God, the people trembled, and could not stand in his presence" (Moses 6:47).

He may have begun with little faith in himself, but spiritual gifts blessed him and he learned of his own potential.

"And so great was the faith of Enoch that he led the people of God, and their enemies came to battle against them; and he spake the word of the Lord, and the earth trembled, and the mountains fled, even according to his command; and the rivers of water were turned out of their course; and the roar of the lions was heard out of the wilderness; and all nations feared greatly, so powerful was the word of Enoch, and so great was the power of the language which God had given him" (Moses 7:13).

In our effort to turn weakness into strength perhaps the greatest question we can ask the Lord is, "Father, show me my part." Can we imagine the marital conflicts and family problems that could be solved quickly if individuals would, in meekness, go to the Lord and ask to be shown their part in the matter? "Lord, show me my part, my responsibility here; what should I do to solve this problem?"

An eighteen-year-old young woman discovered the need to ask this of the Lord when her older brother returned home as the prodigal son after years of absence and a life of complete rebelliousness.

He had experienced a mighty change of heart and had come back to his family, back to the Church, back to the Lord. For her parents it had been a time of great joy and rejoicing. There were tears, there was laughter, there were tender spiritual moments. Parents who had once wept with sorrow were overcome with joy.

Shortly after his return they began to notice a change in their daughter. She was impatient with everyone and grew sullen and distant. It finally occurred to them that she was feeling somewhat threatened. She had been the oldest child at home for many years. Suddenly her brother had displaced her. They knocked on her bedroom door one evening and asked her to visit with them about why she was feeling so hostile.

At first she tried to pretend nothing was wrong, but before long the floodgates opened and she let every emotion tumble unchecked from her guilt-ridden heart.

She had prayed for his return all those years, too. She was glad he was home, after all, it was what everyone wanted. She knew he was sincere, she understood the principle of mercy, but what about justice? She had been a faithful and devoted older sister and daughter the years of his absence. Now she felt that he had stepped in and taken over. What about her obedience? She had never strayed from the commandments. He had done it all, and now, why could he come home and have all restored as before? What good did it do to be faithful if you could sin and then repent and have everything restored again to you?

Her parents tried to reason with her. They told her that the "last chapter" had not been written yet. She would yet see, as the years unfolded, how her obedience would bless her life. Probably, they told her, you will always see the difference in the two of you in some way or another, simply because you chose to be obedient.

She could not be consoled. Finally her parents asked her if she was jealous. At first she protested the question. As they explained the feelings of jealousy to her, armed with the spiritual gifts of understanding and discernment, she admitted verbally that, yes, she was jealous. In that moment, as quickly as she identified her feelings, the feelings left! Once she had a label for her feelings she could do something about them. From that moment on, she struggled slightly a time or two, but the matter had been settled in her heart. She could genuinely welcome her brother home.

5. Spiritual gifts lead us to Christ and help us to feel worthy of his presence as we use the gifts to lift others.

The Savior showed us how to master self-confidence in our labors as he served among his fellowmen and taught that "inasmuch as ye have done it unto one of the least of these my brethren, ye have done it unto me" (Matthew 25:40).

It seems we multiply our potential and confidence and self-reliance as we use spiritual gifts to bless others.

When one of the bishops in our stake was first called to the position, his wife decided to support him by taking a loaf of bread to each new family in their ward. This was a ward that experienced much growth, and almost every week someone new came.

She made bread for her family every Friday. The recipe always made four loaves. But when she began this simple, quiet act of love and service, the recipe somehow began making five loaves. She couldn't understand how this could be, she had never increased the volume of ingredients. This was certainly a type and shadow of what was happening in her own life as she was being led to the Savior. Can you imagine the trust and confidence this gave her in herself and the Lord?

6. Spiritual gifts inspire us to endure to the end.

Our Church buildings don't have physical crosses, but we often believe that we are expected to carry our own. We may perceive those crosses as physical, spiritual, and emotional, or financial burdens. Indeed, it seems impossible at times to carry our cross with one arm, while trying to use the other to hold on to the iron rod.

Self-condemnation and low self-esteem can become especially heavy crosses. Sometimes we have to be the one that refuses to condemn ourselves. Being down on ourselves or allowing discouragement to control us is a destructive situation, the kind that can lead us to perish. If we try to bear this kind of cross it may bury us. That is what it means to perish—to convince ourselves that we are no good, can't make it, can't do it!

But, by asking the Savior to lift our burdens and help us overcome our challenges we can become more than we would have been had we not been burdened at all.

The world philosophy of self-esteem has long deceived many. All our lives we hear that in order for us to do well in life it is crucial that we develop good self-esteem. If we don't feel good about ourselves, how can we have accomplishments and be successful and make good choices? I'm here to tell you that's just not true. The most valuable thing we can teach each other is that no matter how we feel about ourselves, we are expected to make choices that are good, wise, and just. Good choices make us feel good about ourselves.

My father didn't hear the gospel until he was thirty-four

years old. He didn't understand what the worth of souls really meant. He grew up in the worst slums in Houston, Texas. These slums were in an area sandwiched between the polluted bayou and the railroad tracks, far from the city center. There was no indoor plumbing or indoor water supply of any kind. Very few had electricity, most used kerosene lamps. Heat came from a potbelly stove when fuel was obtainable. There was never enough food, and even in this twentieth century United States, there was much hunger. Childhood diseases took many small lives. There was tuberculosis, crime, drugs, alcoholism, and much suffering.

One evening when Dad was nine years old, he was overcome with sorrow as he considered his pitiful existence. He secluded himself in some forgotten little corner by the railroad tracks and began to cry uncontrollably. He wept because he was hungry. He thought of all the suffering around him and the hopelessness of where he lived. He cried out in silent anguish, "Why was I born? Why was I born?"

Immediately, he heard a small voice say to him clearly, "Someday, it will be worth it, you'll see, it will be worth it."

Although he did not know that voice then as he does now, he never forgot it.

Twenty-five years later, when he finally did hear the gospel and read the Book of Mormon, he knew this was why he had been born and that it was going to be worth it.

A missionary named Elder Bushman was determined to endure to the end and also lifted what I can now see must have been somewhat of a cross for him.

He served a mission in 1954. He was from a small community called Sho-Lo, Arizona. He was a retired dairy farmer. This was in the days when men were still called to serve missions without their wives. I can only imagine the sorrow at his parting when he said good-bye to his wife and the security of his little home and community. Perhaps he was seen as unpolished and unsophisticated. He had spent his entire life in the somewhat secluded area of northern Arizona.

But he made a good, wise, and just choice. He accepted the call to serve a six-month mission. He converted only one soul his whole mission. That person was my father. And now, there are forty members of my extended family that are members of the Church and temple work is being done for thousands more in our family.

Little did Elder Bushman know as he dried the tear from his cheek the day he left Sho-Lo that he was being sent to fulfill the Lord's promise to a nine-year-old boy. "It will be worth it. You'll see, it will be worth it."

No, my children do not get a hot dinner every night; some nights I'm not sure what they eat. And more difficult yet, they aren't all keeping the commandments. But I have got to endure to the end. I want to retain and reclaim my children and those many other children around me whom I love. Relying on the Savior and nurturing the spiritual gifts he has granted me is the key I have in order to do so.

We can endure to the end and we can endure it well. Your greatest influence on your children, on all God's children, will be your example. If you want the children to see what the gospel will do for them, let them see what it has done for you.

I met a woman, a young widow with four small children to raise alone, who was learning how spiritual gifts could inspire her to endure to the end.

She was grief stricken after the accidental death of her husband. She was faced with the reality of putting food on the table, paying bills, and caring for these small children, too young to understand the crisis at hand.

One day in frustration she simply blurted out to her mother, "I can't do this!" To which this wise and loving mother responded, "You have to!"

This good woman told me she realized how true this was. She could not change the circumstance, but she could change her attitude. In seeking out the Savior and developing specific spiritual gifts she was succeeding in overcoming her trials.

Even though we aren't fully worthy, we are full of worth. If this were not true, the whole world would have been utterly wasted at the Savior's great sacrifice. He gave his life because he knew many would follow the Shepherd home, holding fast along the path with that rod of iron.

3

THE LORD WILL REMEMBER THE PRAYERS OF THE RIGHTEOUS

*I*t was Christmastime, just a few days before December 25th. A sister from Layton, Utah, welcomed her college children home. Included among the visitors were her recently married son and his bride.

Friday evening after dinner, the young couple told them of their plans to go across the mountain in the morning to a special Christmas fair in Logan, about one hour's drive away. This concerned mother told them to be sure to get up early. A storm was predicted, and she had been over that road enough times in bad weather to know how dangerous it could be. They agreed to leave early and return early.

However, the next morning, everyone slept in until around noon. As her son and daughter-in-law were preparing to leave for the day's outing, this mother looked at the gray skies and felt a little nervous. She asked them to rethink their plans. No, they would be just fine, they said. "Please, Mother, don't worry!" Off they went as she headed for the mall to do last minute shopping.

Pulling into the parking lot, she saw snow flurries and a sudden sense of fear shook her a little. She bowed her head and said a prayer that her children would be safe and use caution. A feeling of calmness came over her, and she dismissed the anxiety for the moment and headed for the stores.

Returning to her car later, the flurries had now turned into lightly falling snow. She knew this meant much worse weather through and over the mountains. Sliding behind the wheel, her heart pounding frantically, she began to feel tremendous fear once more. Then she remembered her prayer and the calmness that had come.

She began to think how foolish she was feeling. She thought back to her own youth and young married days. Why, there were plenty of times in her life that she had been impulsive and impetuous, thinking nothing of the risks. She remembered often jumping in the car and taking off on adventures. She thought to herself, *and see, nothing happened to me.*

As soon as that thought entered her mind, another one entered her heart, and she heard the words, "Yes, and who do you think was praying for you?"

For the first time in her fifty-some years of living, she realized that as she had been praying for her children, throughout her life there had always been someone praying for her. Since the day she was born someone had continually been praying for her. Not a day in her life had passed without prayers for her. Her parents, her grandparents, her husband, her children, ward members, the bishop, the prophet, perhaps even those on the other side of the veil who had gone before or were yet to come. What remarkable thoughts! What comforting remembrance!

"The Lord will remember the prayers of the righteous" (Mormon 5:21). Will we remember to pray? Will we remember to trust in those prayers? Will we believe those righteous prayers are unperishable? Will we perish because we will not pray or we will not believe in prayer?

My young son, Chase, received answers there on an operating table in a cold and frightening hospital room. The Lord even held in reserve weeks of prayers in order to release them to Chase's memory at the appropriate hour.

Many words have been written and spoken about faith. "Faith, if it hath not works, is dead" (James 2:17). Faith without prayer (works) is really of little strength and value to us. But, prayer without faith is just as shallow and useless. Prayers offered up with sincere conviction that God listens become prayers of power.

A sister missionary writes of her experience in learning to pray with honesty and sincerity because of faith in the living God. She wrote of her second night at the Missionary Training Center in Provo:

> I didn't like my companion, I didn't like Spanish, and I didn't like myself much for being such a baby.
>
> I started my prayer, but then realized that I didn't have anything to say. Although I desperately needed someone to talk to, it just didn't seem right to express my empty, lonely, and bitter feelings to Heavenly Father. I finally said a standard, "thank you for my health and the chance to be here," sort of prayer and crawled into bed.
>
> Why doesn't Heavenly Father help me? If he really knows how I feel before I ask, what is he waiting for? I thought angrily.
>
> Then I remembered the book of Enos, which I had read that afternoon. . . . His words echoed in my mind: "I did pour out my whole soul unto God" (Enos 1:9).
>
> Had I done the same? . . . I knew I hadn't.
>
> I knelt again. This time I had plenty to say. I told my Father how frustrated I felt, how I couldn't learn the language, how I needed to love my companion, and how I wanted to do a good job. I cried as I explained that I felt abandoned, and I needed his help. . . .
>
> This time, I didn't say a prayer—I prayed. (Christie Ann Giles, "A Change of Heart," *New Era*, November 1991, p. 11.)

What this young woman expressed was a need for real intent. This is a concern I have as I see many youth who are able to repeat back to us the good and true answers they have been taught all of their lives. They answer correctly, not because they feel it, but because they have learned it. This is not going to be enough to hold on to the rod when their personal mists of darkness come. Without real intent, we are ever learning and never able to come to a knowledge of the truth (see *Discourses of Brigham Young,* comp. John A. Widtsoe [Salt Lake City: Deseret Book Co., 1977], pp. 90–91).

Without real intent we cannot understand the dealings of our God. "And if ye shall ask with a sincere heart, with real intent, having faith in Christ, he will manifest the truth of it unto you, by the power of the Holy Ghost" (Moroni 10:4).

"For behold, God hath said a man being evil cannot do that which is good; for if he offereth a gift, or prayeth unto God, except he shall do it with real intent it profiteth him nothing. . . . And likewise also is it counted evil unto a man, if he shall pray and not with real intent of heart; yea, and it profiteth him nothing, for God receiveth none such." (Moroni 7:6, 9.)

Without real intent, faith in Jesus Christ and in our Father in Heaven becomes a vague and elusive concept instead of a key for each of us to hold more fast to the rod.

Author Stephen E. Robinson has taught that faith really consists of two parts. It is one part of faith to believe in Christ, that he lived, that he is the Savior, that he died and was resurrected, and that he atoned for our sins. It is indeed another part of faith to believe him; to believe him when he says he loves us, to believe him that our worth is great, to believe him when he tells us he is watching over us and "his hand is stretched out still" (2 Nephi 15:25) to bring us safely home.

"And now, behold, I say unto you, and I would that ye should remember, that God is merciful unto all who believe on his name; therefore he desireth, in the first place, that ye should believe, yea, even on his word" (Alma 32:22).

Without believing what the Savior has told us about his role in our lives, we will have less faith and limit how much God can work with us. Can you see how ineffective our prayers will be if we don't believe Christ? Prayer is for us, not God, he already has all the news. Real intent becomes vital when we understand this.

Without the double perspective of faith, we also tend to neglect repentance.

> And thus he shall bring salvation to all those who shall believe on his name; this being the intent on this last sacrifice, to bring about the bowels of mercy, which overpowereth justice, and bringeth about means unto men that they may have faith unto repentance.
>
> And thus mercy can satisfy the demands of justice, and encircles them in the arms of safety, while he that exercises no faith unto repentance is exposed to the whole law of the demands of justice; therefore only unto him that has faith unto repentance is brought about the great and eternal plan of redemption. (Alma 34:15–16.)
>
> But as oft as they repented and sought forgiveness, with real intent, they were forgiven. (Moroni 6:8.)

If we don't believe in Christ and believe Christ that the Atonement is for us because we need it, then we won't have enough faith to repent. Without honest and humble repentance and real intent, we can never grasp an understanding of the Atonement in our lives. Without repentance our faith will continue to weaken. Without repentance there can be no self-esteem. Without repentance prayer becomes less and less honest. Without repentance it is hard to remember "the tender mercies" (1 Nephi 1:20) of the Lord in our lives. Without remembrance we will likely forget the Lord and trample him under our worldly walk. The LDS Bible dictionary describes the Greek word from which the word repentance originates as meaning "a change of mind" (p. 760). Does it always take a change of mind to remember and repent? We let ourselves get away with inappropriate behavior until one day we are so heavy with the burden of ignoring it, that we "change our minds" and repent. To remember the Lord is to change our minds from our worldly thoughts that distract or tempt us away from him.

If we fail or refuse to remember to exercise faith unto repentance, even to change our minds, we will "forget" to pray and we will begin to perish. The true spirit of prayer is based on repentance. "Yea, cry unto him for mercy; for he is mighty to save. Yea, humble yourselves, and continue in prayer unto him." (Alma 34:18–19.)

It is a touching account of the Savior's love and compassion for the Nephites as he visited among them following the great destruction and his appearance as the resurrected Lord. When he is about to depart and leave for a few hours, what is the instruction he leaves them? "I perceive that ye are weak, that ye cannot understand all my words which I am commanded of the Father to speak unto you at this time. Therefore, go ye unto your homes, and ponder upon the things which I have said, and ask of the Father, in my name, that ye may understand, and prepare your minds for the morrow, and I come unto you again." (3 Nephi 17:2–3.)

He was coming back the next day, he was personally present and administering to them. Yet, what did he want them to do? *To remember.* He asked them to remember (ponder) and to pray. Prayers are for us. They strengthen us. They bring power. They allow us to be in a time and place where we can receive instruction, comfort, and knowledge. Prayer helps us to remember the Lord so that we will have his spirit to be with us. "For the Spirit speaketh the truth and lieth not. Wherefore, it speaketh of things as they really are, and of things as they really will be." (Jacob 4:13.)

Nor does the Lord want our mortal lives, our temporal goods, or our families to perish.

Cry unto him when ye are in your fields, yea, over all your flocks.

Cry unto him in your houses, yea, over all your household, both morning, mid-day, and evening.

Yea, cry unto him against the power of your enemies.

Yea, cry unto him against the devil, who is an enemy to all righteousness.

Cry unto him over the crops of your fields, that ye may prosper in them.

Cry over the flocks of your fields, that they may increase.

But this is not all; ye must pour out your souls in your closets, and your secret places, and in your wilderness.

Yea, and when you do not cry unto the Lord, let your heart be full, drawn out in prayer unto him continually for your welfare, and also for the welfare of those who are around you. (Alma 34:20–27.)

The Lord *remembers* the prayers of the righteous.

My friend Chris was a busy and involved Church member—the wife of a stake missionary and mother of six. Life for them was not perfect; there were some financial stresses and the growing pains of a large family. But generally, they seemed to be happy and full of hope and promise of celestial goals.

Then one day Chris's life began to change before her eyes, without her ability to stop it. Her husband decided he loved someone else more; in fact, a woman to whom he had introduced the gospel. There were some serious moral transgressions, and a bitter divorce seemed imminent.

Chris held on, struggling for daily strength, fighting for home, husband, and family. Eventually it became obvious the marriage was over and there would be no reconciliation.

Chris suffered. She wept and drank again and again from the bitter cup. She sought peace and counsel from others, even priesthood blessings. The weeks moved closer to court dates. Her broken heart could not be comforted. She went to the temple, she prayed often, and long and hard.

As the finality became settled in her mind, she sought inner assurance as well. Her mother had passed away when she was a young woman. How she longed for her mother and the consoling hugs and comfort that only a mother can bring.

Alone in the temple one evening her thoughts turned again to her mother. She longed for that hug and silently prayed, "Oh Heavenly Father, if I could just have one hug, one hug from my mother. It's foolish perhaps, but in a way I guess I need to know that somebody still loves me for me."

She felt as if her self-esteem had been temporarily deposited in the divorce courtroom. Just one hug, a little inner assurance of her own worth.

The session came to an end, she moved into the celestial room and found an empty corner. There she retreated into her thoughts and worked with her pain, the tears quietly fell upon white satin.

As if from nowhere, a woman tapped her on the shoulder and Chris looked up. She saw the woman motion to her husband to go on without her, and then she turned to Chris and said, "Say, you look like you need a hug. Can I give you just one hug?"

Can you imagine what a healing moment that must have been?

Some months later Chris faced more weakness, more sorrow not of her own doing. She slipped back into the deadly abyss of self-pity and discouragement, even despair. She wondered if that moment in the temple had even been real. Was she just in the right place at the right time, or was this the loving touch of the Lord? Isn't it interesting how intense sorrow and pain can distort the memory of great moments of truth?

Her Sunday School class was studying the Doctrine and Covenants. One evening she picked up the book, hoping to read something that would bring more of a witness of the

Lord's love for her. She offered up a prayer of hope that the words would lend her strength. She read:

> Verily, verily, I say unto thee, blessed art thou for what thou hast done; for thou hast inquired of me, and behold, as often as thou hast inquired thou hast received instruction of my Spirit. If it had not been so, thou wouldst not have come to the place where thou art at this time.
>
> Behold, thou knowest that thou hast inquired of me and I did enlighten thy mind; and now I tell thee these things that thou mayest know that thou hast been enlightened by the Spirit of truth;
>
> Yea, I tell thee, that thou mayest know that there is none else save God that knowest thy thoughts and the intents of thy heart. . . .
>
> Verily, verily, I say unto you, if you desire a further witness, cast your mind upon the night that you cried unto me in your heart, that you might know concerning the truth of these things.
>
> Did I not speak peace to your mind concerning the matter? What greater witness can you have than from God? (D&C 6:14–16, 22–23.)

What the Lord reminded her to do was to remember, because he had not forgotten her. Her prayers were being heard and answered.

Throughout our earthly stay God protects our experiences from interference. He often is blamed for not intervening. He is often scorned for allowing adversity to occur. Have we ever been tempted to murmur, "Where is God? Doesn't he hear my prayers?"

There are two kinds of experience. There is a lesser kind that we simply live through—a sore throat, a fender bender, misplaced keys, juice spilled on new carpet, or other such stresses that cause turmoil or some level of discomfort. There is a higher kind of experience that we must work through—

a wayward loved one, a difficult illness, a financial crisis, or even a natural disaster.

There are some instances in this life when we don't have a choice about what happens to us. Our choice comes in the way we deal with those circumstances. If we simply choose to live through difficult experiences by murmuring, blaming, complaining, or even exaggerating our suffering for more pity, we will not enjoy the great profitable spiritual experience this life can be. "My son, peace be unto thy soul; thine adversity and thine afflictions shall be but a small moment; and then, if thou endure it well, God shall exalt thee on high" (D&C 121:7–8).

"If the heavens gather blackness, and all the elements combine to hedge up the way; and above all, if the very jaws of hell shall gape open the mouth wide after thee, know thou, my son, that all these things shall give thee experience, and shall be for thy good" (D&C 122:7).

My ten-year-old son kept forgetting his lunch. Day after day, despite many reminders, I would find myself running up to the school at the lunch hour with the little brown bag. I even tried leaving it at the front door. The problem persisted, and I got cross with him; I pleaded with him, left notes. Nothing was working.

He began forgetting homework assignments and other small responsibilities. He was an energetic, normal ten year old, preoccupied with many other adventures like fort building, bicycling, and sports.

One morning I opened the refrigerator and saw the brown bag. As I looked it seemed to take other shapes: a future college term paper, a family in his mission, a career, his own wife and children, Church callings. Would these dependencies on someone else always rescuing him create larger problems in the future? Would his self-reliance be handicapped?

Slowly I closed the refrigerator door, lunch still inside.

I didn't eat lunch that day either. I thought of my little boy who loved his food. He never was hungry, he was always starving! I am sure the pain I felt was worse than the pain of his hunger. When he came in he stormed in, like a miniature tornado, wondering why I hadn't brought his lunch to him, he was starving! He opened the door and devoured it.

We spent the next few minutes talking about his responsibility to take care of his assignments in life. At ten years old, he wasn't responsible for providing food for himself, his parents were. But, at ten years old he was responsible to take his lunch to school. If he could learn to do this, he could be given greater, then greater responsibilities. But it was all his choice. I also assured him I wouldn't be bringing his lunch to school anymore.

He never forgot it again.

In the midst of our earthly experiences our Father in Heaven has to protect our agency so that we can learn deeper principles. The pain he feels at our pain and sorrow must be that of great love and compassion. And it must be intense at times because he knows he could interfere and bring us our "lunch." His pain must be born of restraint. Because of his greater desire for us to have a profitable spiritual experience rather than merely be his puppets, we get the mistaken idea he is not there for us.

He hears and answers every prayer. Some answers are not what we want to hear, so we claim there has been no answer. Some answers come as silence because, as he once told me, "I gave you a brain, now use it!"

My sister and her husband sat in the Las Vegas Temple one Friday afternoon waiting for the next session to start. Her thoughts turned to the sweetness of the spirit she felt, the significance of the covenants she made, and the love and unity she felt with her husband. She began to feel a desire that she and her husband could be the witness couple. They had never been a witness couple before.

She struggled with that thought, wondering if it was right to desire that. She considered praying and asking that the

brother in charge would be inspired to select them. Then she
told herself that they probably wouldn't select them, especially because her husband had long hair!

Instantly a voice came into her mind, and she heard these
words: "Your Heavenly Father knows the righteous desires of
your heart even before you ask for them in prayer." Even before that sentence was completed, a temple worker was standing over them and asking if they would like to be the witness
couple at this session.

I had to fly to Mexico City one Thursday evening to in-
spect a project site under my design direction. The clients
were leaving on Saturday for a two-month tour of their facto-
ries in Europe and the Orient, and there were dozens of questions to be resolved with them and the contractors that Friday.
It had been a last minute request on their part, and my trip
was going to be an overnight, but very intense, visit.

I arrived at the hotel around midnight and went immediately to sleep. Around three o'clock in the morning I was
awakened by an excruciating, stabbing pain in my mouth with
what would be classified as an extreme dental emergency.

My husband had done some dental work on me earlier in
the week in preparation for further work the next week. I was
in excruciating pain. I didn't know what to do. A million dollars of decisions were resting on me the next day. I had to be
clearminded and alert, especially with the language barrier;
my Spanish is only adequate and requires great concentration
on my part.

My first thought was to call my husband and get the name
of a drug that would stop the pain. Then I worried that it
wouldn't be the same dosage or type in Mexico. Then I wondered if the concierge would be able to find someone at three
o'clock in the morning to even obtain it. And then, with complete realization, it occurred to me that any drug strong
enough to knock out this pain would completely knock me out,
and I would be useless the next day. I didn't know what to do.

Then came the distinct and clear message: "You have faith. You know what to do."

I climbed out of bed, knelt in prayer, and told the Lord of my situation and all that had concerned me, and asked him to please take away the pain long enough for me to complete my work the next day. Before I said "in the name of Jesus Christ, amen," the pain vanished. Instantly, in a moment, it was gone. I thanked him and went back to sleep.

The next day I was able to answer the questions, make urgent and very critical decisions, and finish on time to catch my flight home. By the time I was in customs in Los Angeles, the pain was returning. When I landed in Las Vegas several hours later, I had another full-blown dental emergency!

But this is not the whole story. Two days later was fast Sunday. In our monthly family testimony meeting I told of my experience and my witness of the power of faith and prayer.

My fifteen-year-old son grew amazed. I could see his countenance change. When I finished speaking he asked, "Mom, was this Thursday night?"

"Yes," I said.

"And was it about two o'clock in the morning?"

I thought about that, it was three o'clock in Mexico, but with the hour time change I told him it was two o'clock in Las Vegas.

Suddenly he was filled with emotion and told me the beginning of the story. He had been awakened at two o'clock in the morning that night with a voice that said, "Your mother is in trouble, pray for her." He had slipped out of bed, and on his knees, with real intent, had said, "Heavenly Father, my mom has faith. Tell her what to do."

The Lord heard his prayer and reminded his mother of her faith and that she knew what to do.

Another mother, in a reverse role, prayed from her righteous heart for her teenage son who struggled spiritually. At the time, he was away from home, with some loved ones who were trying to help him chart a new course and correct his direction. He was willing to accept the help. In fact, he wanted to be a part of better things, but he was struggling with giving up old habits.

She sat one evening pondering what she could pray for that would be the most powerful influence in his young life. She thought of many ideas, but nothing was specific, until she actually got on her knees and began to pray. Then into her mind came the words of people who had heard King Benjamin's address: "And they all cried with one voice, saying: Yea, we believe all the words which thou hast spoken unto us; and also, we know of their surety and truth, because of the Spirit of the Lord Omnipotent, which has wrought a mighty change in us, or in our hearts, that we have no more disposition to do evil, but to do good continually" (Mosiah 5:2). She asked the Lord to bless her son with people and thoughts and experiences that would inspire him to lose the disposition to do evil and be filled with a desire to do good continually.

After her prayer she opened the Book of Mormon and read that entire chapter and found much more to pray for in behalf of her son. She prayed that he would remember he had taken the name of Jesus Christ upon him and that he would remember there was no other way salvation could come, and she prayed that when he returned home he would be "steadfast and immovable" in his commitment of a new heart (see Mosiah 5:8–15).

Several months passed, and he told his parents he was ready to come home, he had much to tell them. He had experienced some events that caused him to have a new heart. He had the desire to do good forever and he felt repulsed at what he had partaken of before.

My daughter Ashley served her mission in the Hawaiian Islands. She had been assigned to the visitors' center at the temple in Laie on the island of Oahu. Halfway through her mission she was assigned to full-time proselytizing on the smaller island of Kauai. She and her companion were located in a small and somewhat remote area on this island.

The little branch they worked with was tucked away in this breathtakingly beautiful little corner of the islands. The time there was difficult because there was almost no one to teach. She felt discouragement because the work was so slow, so meager. She and her companion decided that they would create work. They decided to focus on the less-active families in the branch.

They made personal visits to these families and went around with a plan. When the door opened, here stood two lovely, radiant young women who introduced themselves as sister missionaries. Then they explained they had no one to teach the gospel to and were afraid they would forget their discussions, could they practice on this family?

Two bubbly, petite, and radiant young twenty-one-year-old girls would be hard to refuse and have to face their looks of rejection. They were able to get in all the doors they petitioned.

A "marvelous work and a wonder" took place the seven months she was there. Many came back.

Week after week she wrote of one particular family that I will call the Clays. Week after week we saw her love and hope grow for them. Week after week we looked forward to her report of their progress.

The Clays had been less active for many, many years. They had been married and divorced from each other three times. They were currently living together, but not married. They had three little girls.

Their lives had been filled with drug abuse and addiction, alcoholism, and other serious spiritual problems. They were struggling physically, emotionally, and spiritually.

As Ashley and her companion came to bring the gospel back into their home, it was the wife who responded first. She had not been to church since she was thirteen or fourteen. The husband had not participated since he had been a teenager as well.

At the first meeting in their home, Brother Clay acknowledged the sister missionaries with a somewhat cool greeting, and then he left the room. Sister Clay listened to their discussion and responded positively enough to invite them to return. At the second visit she informed them he wasn't interested, he didn't want anything to do with the Church at all. That would be fine with them, Ashley told her, she was glad to be able to "practice" at least with Sister Clay.

Week after week they faithfully returned. Week after week they saw small changes taking place in Sister Clay. Her faith was rekindled, the flicker of a testimony began to be fanned back into a flame. She began to come to sacrament meeting. She began to bring her girls. She looked forward to the meetings with the sister missionaries. She spoke of her desires to return to the gospel. She began to be filled with real intent.

One visit became a turning point for Brother Clay. Ashley had the opportunity to ask him if he would join them. He was extremely negative and told her that the Church had been pushed at him too hard and that it had been more important to others than he was. He wanted nothing to do with it or the priesthood. At that opportunity she told him what the priesthood had meant to her.

Now imagine this: standing in front of him was a tiny five-foot-two young woman, who probably appeared to him to be about sixteen or seventeen, who was filled with humility and radiating love. She began to speak of her years at home and her life of personal struggles. She spoke of specific experiences and specific counsel and priesthood blessings from her dad. She told Brother Clay that she couldn't imagine her life without this guidance and security. She told him how much it had meant to her to have a father who was worthy so that she could call upon him anytime for blessings of comfort and peace and courage. She expressed her feelings of gratitude and love for her father and how much his guidance and priesthood leadership had meant to her. She concluded by telling him she wondered where she would be now without it, probably not in Hawaii or on a mission. He had three daughters, she testified of the blessing the priesthood could be to them.

She watched the stiff defensiveness in his physical posture begin to relax. His face began to reveal that he was pondering her words. She felt a quiet spirit about him. She knew he was considering his own three young and adorable daughters. This time he listened to their discussion.

The next Sunday he came to church, and the Sunday after that, and kept coming Sunday after Sunday. At first they only stayed for sacrament meeting. He came in Aloha shirts and jeans and thongs.

One day a letter came from Ashley filled with excitement and joy. She was writing the day after fast and testimony meeting. Guess who, she wrote, had stood that morning and borne his testimony? Brother Clay! He had come to church in a new suit, white shirt, tie, and shoes. He had gone to the pulpit and borne his testimony that he knew the Church is true and wanted to come back fully. Then she wrote of a specific sentence he had said about her. Then she wrote: "Oh by the way, Mom, his mother knows you. You stayed in their home when you spoke in their stake. It was the stake where (and she cited a familiar name) was the stake president."

This startled me. I began to remember that visit nearly six years earlier. If Ashley had not named the stake president, I would never have been able to recall this experience with Brother Clay's parents. I remembered those parents, even the room I stayed in. The memories came flooding back.

During that talk I had shared hope and feelings of love for my own wayward, lost son. I spoke that day of hope and prayer and of a God who does hear and answer our prayers.

Brother Clay's parents drove me back to the airport after the conference. During that ride, they poured out their hearts to me of their love and hope for a son who had been gone from them and from the Church for many years. They had not even seen him in a long time. He was living in some remote village in the Hawaiian Islands.

They spoke of serious and sorrowful experiences with

drugs and alcohol and the law. I didn't remember the details but I did remember their sorrow and I remembered the gravity of their son's situation. They even had a grandchild they had never seen. There seemed to be no hope, even after years of praying.

I remembered what happened next. There was a wonderful spirit in the car as we spoke and shared thoughts. Then suddenly, without forethought, I found myself saying and promising to them that one day there would come into their son's life someone who would touch his heart, and he would change!

I remember wondering later where that had come from. I had hoped it was the Spirit, I worried I had said the wrong thing.

It was Ashley's letter, and the mention of the stake president's name that brought it all back. But it was the comment in Brother Clay's testimony of a loving God who remembers the prayers of the righteous that filled my heart with remembrance.

He had stood and said, "When Sister Canfield came into my home, she touched my heart, and I wanted to change."

Who would have ever known six years before when I told this to his parents it would be my daughter? Of all the places in the world she could have been sent, and of all the places in Hawaii she could have served, it was in this tiny, secluded area where the Lord knew the address of this righteous couple's son. Coincidence? I don't think so. Riding in that car six years ago, my daughter at home was only sixteen years old. I believe the Lord allowed Ashley and me to be a part of this witness that he is in charge. He knows his flock, the ones who have strayed and the ones who pray for them. His "hand is stretched out still," and even if we think it isn't, it is!

There was a program on public television recently that explored the question of the existence of angels. The historical genre of angels was first presented, followed by theories and philosophies. The program concluded by having people share their stories of what they believed were experiences with angels. There is a story in our family that could have been related on that program, and we discussed it that night.

But it wasn't until later the next day that I thought about the many angels that have touched my life over the years. They weren't unseen beings, but flesh and blood individuals who were, like Chris's "angel" in the temple, delivering answers to prayers.

Many years ago I lived in a ward where there was a tradition to bring dinners to the family of a sister who had just delivered a new baby. Her first night home from the hospital she was greeted by visiting teachers and a complete dinner.

One evening, about three days after we got Paige through the adoption process, my doorbell rang. There stood my friend Karma Earl on my porch with dinner. I asked her what was going on, to which she replied, "Well, you just had a new baby, didn't you? You have to have your welcome home dinner." I protested, telling her that I didn't actually give birth. I told her that in fact I was already preparing dinner. She walked right past me into the kitchen; assorted children followed, carrying dishes behind her.

Then, she turned and said, "It's orange glazed chicken, seven-layer salad, steamed rice, vegetables, homemade rolls, and baked Alaska for dessert. This was not a tuna casserole effort because it is made with real love for you and your family. Anita, you are a new mother, whether you gave birth or not, and I wanted to honor you like we do all new mothers."

It wasn't just the food that strengthened me that night. It was my angel that brought a message of sisterhood to me from the Lord.

There is one other angel that will be in my memory for eternity. Her name is Candy Marsh.

She was a less-active sister who had been my visiting teacher for six or seven months. She liked visiting teaching and found that this was something she felt comfortable doing. She was full of life and joy and creativity. Often the visits turned into gospel instruction in which she asked questions and I tried to answer them.

My oldest son had been involved in drugs and alcohol. He was only sixteen at the time and after a restless weekend he packed up and left home. That day I felt the Spirit impress upon me that I should brace myself, he wasn't coming home to live ever again.

That sorrow was the worst pain I had ever experienced. So great was the pain that I could not bear to think on the situation for long but could only linger on memories of his birth, my hopes and dreams when I held him for the first time. I saw him as a toddler, as a curious little boy, as an eight year old in white at his baptism. I mentally beat myself up for my mistakes with him. All of this while trying to console his broken-hearted younger brother and sister.

Three or four days passed and I was supposed to withdraw him from school. I called and asked if I could do it by phone. No, they said, I had to come in person.

I had been praying for forgiveness for any of my part in his leaving. At the time it seemed that perhaps it had been all my fault. I had been praying for some kind of assurance that the Lord knew us and would have mercy on our little family.

I got in my car and headed for the school. About a block away, I turned down a side street. I couldn't bring myself to do it just yet. It would be a final severance and I knew it. The Holy Ghost had warned me, he wasn't coming back.

Suddenly in my mind came the words, "Go see Candy Marsh." I dismissed them just as quickly as they had entered my thoughts. No, I certainly didn't want to see anyone. I continued to drive through the neighborhood trying vainly to get my car to head towards the school.

Again came the thought, "Go see Candy Marsh." And I argued, why should I go see her? She comes to me for gospel answers. There isn't anything she could tell me that would be of real comfort.

Again, for the third time, "Go see Candy Marsh." A few minutes later, I found myself knocking on her front door.

She wondered why I had come. I told her I needed to use her phone. She raised her eyebrows and queried, "Yours doesn't work?" I made an excuse, and she invited me in.

I called the school and questioned them as to whether I had all the paperwork I needed to withdraw him. When I hung up, she asked me if something had happened and I found myself telling her the entire detailed events of the preceding year right up to that moment, including confessing my feelings of weakness as his mother. I was too numb by this time to shed tears, just the grim explanation of great sorrow.

Then, as if with angelic countenance, she told me of her own life as a young girl. She related some experiences that I realize now, no other person could have told me in such a manner that I could have accepted. She then said, "Anita, no child can refuse the gifts a mother gives. They may look like it and act like it for a while, but the Lord won't permit them to be able to refuse a mother's gifts. Despite the mistakes we make as mothers, we have spiritual gifts that bless our child forever. They never are able to refuse those gifts."

She blessed me eternally that day. The Lord had answered the exact prayer I had asked. I was comforted and understood that we are never alone. Angels are with us.

Remember the story of Elisha the prophet having the king of Syria in hot pursuit of him? Elisha's young servant got up early one morning to find themselves and the city surrounded by an army of chariots and horses of the king of Syria. He was terrified and asked Elisha what they were going to do. To which Elisha responded: "Fear not: for they that be with us are more than they that be with them." And the servant's eyes were opened and he saw "the mountain was full of horses and chariots of fire round about Elisha" (2 Kings 6:16–17).

Our missionary daughter wrote of lofty goals of increasing the number of referrals at the temple visitors' center. The average had been around two hundred per month. The goal had been raised to four hundred and fifty.

Monday afternoon tours are the slowest for the entire week, and Ashley knew this the Monday that she witnessed the miracle of prayer again.

That morning she had awakened with a strong desire to give the tours and an overwhelming feeling of love for the gospel. She was filled with the desire that those taking the tours would have the chance to hear the gospel and partake of it.

She prayed that Heavenly Father would inspire people to just come on the grounds so that she would even be able to give tours. She prayed that they would be inspired to take the tours. She went to work.

From ten o'clock that morning until four thirty that afternoon, six and a half hours, the tours were filled to capacity. For every tour she prayed for specific things for each person. She prayed that visitors would be referrals so that the missionaries could come to their homes and they could have the blessings of the gospel.

As the hours wore on, she had such a love for all these strangers from many lands—her prayers became more and more specific.

At the end of the day everyone on her tours, without exception, had requested the missionaries to come to their respective homes! And, at the end of that month, the overall goal had been surpassed. The goal had been four hundred and fifty and they actually reached seven hundred and seventy!

She wrote: "I know faith and prayer is the greatest power . . . it's so easy to do, but it does take effort and hard work, but if the desire is there, the desire to bring souls unto Christ or whatever the situation is, if there is a sincere desire, God does hear and answer prayers." In other words, we need real intent.

I was a young woman when the ill-fated Apollo 13 mission became the focus of millions of prayers in their behalf. The television stations broadcast the gathering of thousands in every part of the world, and we could see heads bowed in humility and real intent. My heart stirred as I realized the whole world was praying for their safe return. I wonder how great a global sight that was for Heavenly Father to see.

The precarious window of opportunity for their safe return was so slight that I have no doubt these prayers were answered, and angels helped steer that craft.

My friend Dev had a struggle with her oldest son. She watched helplessly as he deliberately pursued a path of drugs and alcohol. As he neared mission age, he became more rebellious, and there were problems with the law.

As he approached his twenty-first year, she began to pray more specifically. She began to request that others who would be able to have an influence on her son would be inspired to visit him.

Soon, friends, ward members, and others started mentioning that they had felt impressed to visit him. But once arriving, they all were either turned away or the music was too loud or he simply wasn't home.

Dev didn't let this dissuade her. Instead she prayed more frequently and more specifically. She asked that if her son couldn't be reached during his waking hours, that the Lord would come to him in his sleep.

Months passed and then one evening he came home and walked into the house and announced that he was going on a mission. He had just been to see the bishop, and it would take a while, probably a year, but he was going.

Then he explained. He had been having strange dreams for weeks, dreams about the family and the Church. But the previous night he had a dream which he felt he had really been a part of. This is in his own words:

On July 3, 1990 I had a dream . . . this one was different. It was so *real*. I could smell, hear, feel, see, and even almost taste my surroundings. It wasn't a long dream, nor a very involved or intricate dream. In fact, the only thing significant about this dream were my thoughts, feelings, and actions during and after it.

I was at work. I formerly worked as a lifeguard at the Riviera Hotel, and I was walking up to the desk where we pass out towels. In the dream there was something weighing heavy on my mind, I sensed that something was wrong and on the mind of everyone else there also. No sooner had these thoughts crept into my mind when all of a sudden, everything—the people, footsteps, the slow hum of the electric generators—*everything* went silent. It seemed an eternity before anything happened. During this long period of silence and thought, many thoughts passed through my mind. I had never been so scared in my life. The sun went black. In fact it was as if the sun was swallowed. Even as if the whole earth had been swallowed.

I mentioned my other senses. Allow me to describe to you what else I experienced. I saw the sun darken and I also felt it. It got cold, really cold. I felt alone. There was a smell of tears and a taste of salt in my throat. At that moment I knew that my time was up. That everyone's time was up. That in three short days the Lord would come in all his glory. I realized that I had to go see the bishop, but at the same time the darkness that engulfed and enveloped me wouldn't allow me to see two inches in front of my face, much less would it allow me to find my way to his house.

I fell to my knees and then to my belly and wept. When I woke up I continued to weep. I realized then how I would feel at that moment if I did not repent. Immediately I dropped to my knees and began to pray—praying my heart out to my Father in Heaven and begging for his forgiveness. I went back to sleep that night with my heart ablaze with the knowledge that my Heavenly Father loves me still even though I had forsaken the commandments which he had given us. Even though I had not magnified my priesthood calling and especially that I had ignored the promptings of the Holy Ghost. He still loves me enough to send me this wonderful and horrid dream.

This young man did leave about one year later, served a full-time mission, and now has a temple marriage and family. The Lord heard his mother's prayer and remembered her little family.

The Lord remembers the prayers of the righteous. Will we remember to pray that we might not perish in the difficulties of darker days ahead? Do we believe him when he says he remembers us?

I was in the temple one morning and found myself seated at the end of a row. Next to me, in the aisle, was a very young woman in a wheelchair. She was unable to stand and had to be assisted in everything. She appeared to have full feeling of her body and yet was experiencing extreme physical weakness.

During the prayer the temple officiator said words to this effect: "There are those in this room who are in need of thy healing hands. Remember them with health, Father, as they remember to turn to thee."

I heard soft sobbing coming from this young patron. But I felt a sweet power fill the room and was impressed with the love God has for his sons and daughters and that he waits for us patiently to remember to turn to him.

4

REMEMBER THE WORDS OF YOUR GOD

Behold, my beloved . . .
remember the words of your God;
pray unto him continually by day,
and give thanks unto his holy name by night.
—2 Nephi 9:52

*I*t is one thing to believe *in* Jesus Christ and an entirely different matter to *believe him* when he says he can save us. For most of us it is easy to believe there is a Savior and that Jesus is that Savior. Why is it so much harder for us to have faith in his sacrifice and in his words of eternal life? Many find it so much more difficult to believe they are really worth the price he paid and that he is presently about his task of saving us. We struggle for that eternal perspective to picture ourselves with him one day.

As simple as it sounds, and as often as the prophets counsel, it is true: searching the scriptures cultivates that eternal perspective. "Search the scriptures; for in them ye think ye have eternal life" (John 5:39). As we read and search and ponder, we think more upon these things. Through consistent studying of the scriptures we will think about, we will remember, we will gain a picture of ourselves with him again one day. "Ye ought to search the scriptures. . . . I would ask if ye had read the scriptures? If ye have, how can ye disbelieve on the Son of God?" (Alma 33:2, 14.) In the scriptures we will gain knowledge, even knowledge of who we really are. If we fail to learn who we are—fail to learn our great worth, so great that the Savior gave his life—we shall be "ever learning, and never able to come to the knowledge of the truth" (2 Timothy 3:7).

Nephi taught that the rod of iron was the word of God (see 1 Nephi 11:25) and that the "mists of darkness are the temptations of the devil, which blindeth the eyes, and hardeneth the hearts . . . and leadeth them away into broad roads, that they perish and are lost" (1 Nephi 12:17).

It is not enough to have a belief of our premortal existence. Nor is it enough to have knowledge of our mortal existence and the plan of salvation because Satan is constantly trying to surround us with "mists of darkness" that would cloud our clear view of the road home. We have to gain belief and knowledge that exaltation is not only possible, it is probable because the Savior is hard at work assisting us.

The purpose and spiritual processes of this life can be completely brought into focus and illuminated only by true doctrine. Without that constant and consistent focusing and illumination, the line between this life and eternal perspective becomes unclear and indistinguishable. We even risk becoming "slow to remember the Lord your God" (1 Nephi 17:45). We even risk becoming blinded by the temptations of the devil. Whether they be temptations of doubt, despair, commission, or omission. If we cannot see, we will perish.

We have all seen it. The great and noble members who fall hard. They didn't have eternal perspective. Their spiritual lenses became unfocused. The clear line between eternal perspective and worldly desires became blurred and very undefined. They let go of the rod in a confounding mist of darkness.

King Benjamin's exhortation to his sons to remember serves to give us a sober and sufficiently clear warning of our deep need to remember by searching the scriptures.

My sons, I would that ye should remember that were it not for these plates, which contain these records and these commandments, we must have suffered in ignorance. . . .

For it were not possible that our father, Lehi, could have remembered all these things, to have taught them to his children, except it were for the help of these plates. . . .

. . . Were it not for these things, which have been kept and preserved by the hand of God, that we might read and understand of his mysteries, and have his commandments always before our eyes, that even our fathers would have dwindled in unbelief, and we should have been like unto our brethren, the Lamanites, who know nothing concerning these things, or even do not believe them when they are taught them. . . .

O my sons, I would that ye should remember that these sayings are true, and also that these records are true. . . .

. . . I would that ye should remember to search them diligently, that ye may profit thereby; and I would that ye should keep the commandments of God, that ye may prosper in the land according to the promises which the Lord made unto our fathers. (Mosiah 1:3–7.)

The Prophet Joseph Smith taught that unless the Saints of God, "have an actual knowledge that the course they are pursuing is according to the will of God they will grow weary in their minds, and faint" (*Lectures on Faith,* comp. N. B. Lundwall [Salt Lake City: Bookcraft, n.d.], p. 57). In other words, they will *forget,* and perish.

Searching the scriptures provides practice in cultivating eternal perspective. We can see through them, much like a Urim and Thummim, to the golden portal just beyond our mortal view.

Elder Maxwell writes: "With such intellectual and spiritual nourishment, we can not only rejoice, but, significantly, we will also 'be filled with love towards God and all men' (Mosiah 2:4). People fatigue is dissipated by love and learning: 'And it came to pass that peace and the love of God was restored again among the people; and they searched the scriptures' (Jacob 7:23). Marvelous outcomes flow from inspired insights from the Spirit of scripture. Refreshment, renewal, and reassurance follow. There is also a keener sense, on our part, that we are in fact surrounded 'with so great a cloud of witnesses' (Hebrews 12:1). We become a part of a vast community of believers that transcends time and space, providing precious perspective." (*Meekness and Lowliness* [Salt Lake City: Deseret Book Co., 1987], pp. 41–42.)

To me, it is a wonderful thing to be part of so "vast a community of believers." We are comforted, we are not alone. Many before us have struggled to overcome the world. Many struggle with us. And there are many other struggles yet ahead.

We cannot control much of the external circumstances around us. If we were to depend on physical ability alone to be victorious, we would soon see an end to hope in the world. We will conquer with our minds and our hearts. Our thoughts will fortify us.

If we will read the scriptures, we will begin to think about them. That thinking will change our thoughts, which will in turn change our attitudes and feelings. Even if we don't always understand them, or even if we don't remember much of what we read, the Lord will use our memory, our minds, our thoughts, our remembrance, even the impression of those memories to recall to us those words in times of need. He does truly "speak" to his children so that we will not perish. But he speaks to us in his language—the language of the scriptures, the language of the soul.

Think about what would have happened to Joseph Smith had he not been one who turned diligently to scriptures to see the correct direction. "If any of you lack wisdom, let him ask of God, that giveth to all men liberally, and upbraideth not; and it shall be given him. But let him ask in faith, nothing wavering. For he that wavereth is like a wave of the sea driven with the wind and tossed." The words of James 1:5–6 not only affected him that day, but today they are affecting the entire world in one way or another, reaching out in a massive gospel network of peace that continues to enlarge, eventually encompassing every nation, kindred, tongue, and people.

What about a young man who struggled with the desire and guilt to overcome his homosexuality? His life is different today because he turned to the scriptures as an iron rod to help him as he blindly groped through a mist of darkness. The Lord spoke to him one night as he read: "But behold, he did deliver them because they did humble themselves before him; and because they cried mightily unto him he did deliver them out of bondage; and thus doth the Lord work with his power *in all cases* among the children of men, extending the arm of mercy towards them that put their trust in him" (Mosiah 29:20; emphasis added).

This boy didn't instantly feel heterosexual, but he suddenly felt the overwhelming love of the Savior for him personally. He knew the Savior wanted him, wanted him with all his foolishness, frailties, and weaknesses. It was true! The Savior wanted him! He was taught that night in the classroom of the Spirit of his need to humble himself and "cry mightily" unto the Lord. He learned that he needed to study and understand what trust in the Lord means. He began to see greater strength in his ability to tighten his grip on the rod of iron.

Today his heart has changed. His attitude has changed. He's working on it. He is a worthy son of God. The struggles continue, but the commitment is in place.

What about the young woman who similarly struggles with homosexuality? She felt filthy. She felt unfit to even associate with women whom she perceived to be better than herself. She fed her damaged soul with mortal food until she was dangerously obese. Sorrow, guilt, and shame were her daily visitors.

She had ignored the admonishment in her patriarchal blessing to read and study the Book of Mormon daily. To read it not just once, but over and over again. She was counseled to search the scriptures and warned to never waver from this sacred admonition.

When it felt like her soul could no longer continue to maintain it's existence alone, in her weakest moment, she contemplated suicide. A voice or prompting came to read the Book of Mormon. In a halfhearted, desperate, last-ditch attempt for a spark of hope, she began at chapter one, verse one. In the closing verse of that chapter, the Lord spoke to her. "I, Nephi, will show unto you that the tender mercies of the Lord are over all those whom he hath chosen, because of their faith, to make them mighty *even unto the power of deliverance*" (1 Nephi 1:20; emphasis added).

She was not instantly healed, but she instantly saw the love of God for her individually. She was inspired to continue on, to pursue that healing, to endure to the end. She gained in that message a glimpse of eternity. Eternal perspective was rekindled. She could actually see the iron rod through the dark mist and grabbed hold firmly.

What about the young woman who struggled with some sobering counsel from her parents over a life-changing decision? She had always been eager to listen to their advice and valued their wisdom. Most of the serious decisions in the crossroads of her life had been gospel directed and her life was in harmony with the Lord.

Now she found herself at another crossroads. She had sought their advice but later admitted that what she really wanted was for them to agree with her decision. These parents did not agree with her and counseled her against such a foolish move.

She stubbornly resisted the tender feelings of her parents and their concern for her. But because she had been able to see the results of spiritual direction many times in her life, she turned to the scriptures for further enlightenment. In so doing, the Lord spoke to her as she read. "Now, we will compare the word unto a seed. Now, if ye give place, that a seed may be planted in your heart, behold, if it be a true seed, or a good seed, if ye do not cast it out by your unbelief, that ye will resist the Spirit of the Lord, behold, it will begin to swell within your breasts; and when you feel these swelling motions, ye will begin to say within yourselves—It must needs be that this is a good seed, or that the word is good, for it beginneth to enlarge my soul; yea, it beginneth to enlighten my understanding." (Alma 32:28.)

She saw "the word" as "parents' counsel," and her heart began to soften. She decided that if she followed their counsel, if it was the best advice, the "seed" would swell in her heart and she would soon see the results.

Several years have passed, and she looks back at that time and sees all that she has accomplished and experienced, including a temple marriage. None of this would have been possible if she had not followed her parents' counsel.

What of the young father concerned about his counsel to his children? This man had come from a troubled home where his father had reigned as tyrant and king. There had been tremendous physical and verbal abuse. This young father of three was determined not to repeat this in the family he was now responsible for. He had vowed that the poisonous cycle of abuse would end with him. He would not pass such heinous behavior on.

At first, his attitude in parenting was so passive, he did nothing to help his children with inappropriate behavior. He was so afraid of stepping back into the old familial patterns of tyranny that he chose to simply do nothing. His wife gently persuaded him to seek a better way, to ask for the Lord's help. This young, well-meaning, dedicated, trusting father turned to the scriptures and the Lord spoke to him one day as he read: "No power or influence can or ought to be maintained by virtue of the priesthood, only by persuasion, by long-suffering, by gentleness and meekness, and by love unfeigned; by kindness . . . reproving betimes with sharpness, when moved upon by the Holy Ghost; and then showing forth afterwards an increase of love toward him whom thou hast reproved, lest he esteem thee to be his enemy; that he may know that thy faithfulness is stronger than the cords of death" (D&C 121:41–44). He felt the power of the Holy Ghost bear witness of the eternal truths contained in these verses. He studied and searched the meaning of the word *betimes* and discovered it did not mean "time to time," but that it meant "early on" or "right away." He learned a deeper definition of the word *sharpness* that had nothing to do with harshness, but rather with focus and clarity. And he saw, and tried to emulate, the example of the Savior in the many times he corrected others, right away, before it was too far out of control, and did it with a clear counsel of the problem and how to correct it. Then he remembered the increase of love the Savior always extended to those whom he corrected.

Now his children are grown, but he remains their beloved father and friend. They continue to seek him in times of need. They know they can trust him and that his love for them and faith in God is "stronger than the cords of death." Where there once were many in his lineage who wandered on broad roads, now there are many who hold to the rod.

What about the woman whose husband left her with seven children and no money while he squandered it all on a younger woman? What he did was, indeed, inexcusable. He left behind a trail of tears and eight broken hearts—innocent victims of one man's selfishness. Many serious problems and repercussions grew from one foolish man's choices.

This woman could not be comforted. A year passed and not only was there no change in her heart, there was a growing bitterness and pride. She repeated over and over the offenses in her mind and to anyone that would listen. She wearied her friends and loved ones. She eagerly informed newcomers to the ward. She played the woeful music of self-pity until the sound became like tinkling brass. And yet, she never felt much better.

Until one night. She picked up her scriptures after a long absence from them, and the Lord spoke to her as she read:

"Ye ought to forgive one another; for he that forgiveth not his brother his trespasses standeth condemned before the Lord; for there remaineth in him the greater sin. I, the Lord, will forgive whom I will forgive, but of you it is required to forgive all men. And ye ought to say in your hearts—let God judge between me and thee, and reward thee according to thy deeds." (D&C 64:9–11.) Her understanding awakened when she learned the lesson that it was more of a sin to be offended than to do the offending. She was required to forgive. It would be difficult, but she had to repent.

That forgiveness didn't come overnight. Diligence in asking for help to forgive him did, but not the literal healing.

One morning, months later, as she knelt in sincere and humble prayer, she realized at once that the desire to have him punished was gone! Now, many years later she can testify of how the Savior healed her heart as she has seen and shouldered her responsibility to seek that forgiveness.

And what of the mother who saw her beautiful teenage daughter slipping away into the consuming quicksand of vanity? Her daughter had up until now always been spiritually minded and easily entreated. She was being distracted by her good looks, her popularity, and all the worldly attention she was receiving because of them. She was beginning to value the praises of men more than the approval of the Lord.

This concerned mother turned to the scriptures and found a voice of warning. She fasted and pleaded with the Lord to prepare her daughter to receive these things in heart and mind. The following Sunday the humble mother counseled with her precious child and entreated her to pray with her. After this young woman heard and felt the tenderness so lovingly expressed by the voice of a caring mother speaking in her behalf to God the Eternal Father, she felt humbled and was prepared to give her full attention with an open mind and an open heart to her mother's thoughts.

Mother to daughter, sister to sister, friend to friend, woman to woman, the mother spoke to her of sacred things and of her concern not only for her own priceless daughter, but for all the precious daughters of God. She told her of the great sorrow that is caused when the daughters of God marry the sons of men and lose their inheritance. She spoke of divine responsibility and of the principle where much is given, much is required (see D&C 82:3). And then, in conclusion, she turned to the scriptures and asked her daughter to read a certain verse. The Lord spoke to this tender teenage girl as she read: "And thus we can plainly discern, that after a people have been once enlightened by the Spirit of God, and have had great knowledge of things pertaining to righteousness, and then have fallen away into sin and transgression, they become more hardened, and thus their state becomes worse than though they had never known these things" (Alma 24:30).

Her heart was touched. She saw how easily she was allowing herself to be desensitized to the promptings of the Spirit. She began anew from that moment on and corrected the slight error in her course, resolving to guide the vessel of her soul onward through the narrow strait, and gripped the rod a little stronger.

And what of the two sisters immersed in a fever of strife and malicious envy and contention with their older sister? Petty problems had escalated into giant jealousies. The two younger sisters had begun to project some of their own insecurities and weaknesses onto the older sister, searching for a scapegoat, who for a long time remained oblivious to the growing storm of disdain her sisters held for her.

One evening it exploded, detonating into a fallout of hate. The two sisters, along with their husbands, sat at a table across from the older one and proceeded to hold court against her. They produced a sheet of paper that had been completely covered line by line with their long pent-up grievances.

The accusations included statements of her lust for control, her need to be the heroine, her desire to be in the limelight, her materialism, her manipulation of others in order to enslave them as her puppets. The list was long and detailed.

Last, but not least was the startling declaration that she was not a good mother to her children.

It was a shock to this sister who dearly loved her sisters. Why, she asked, why did they feel this way? Horrified, she professed innocence at their accusations, which made them become even more agitated and hostile. She begged their forgiveness. They told her she had been responsible for their unhappiness. Her weaknesses were making them all miserable. She was responsible for their misery. She struggled to find some stable ground, but, feeling suffocated and overpowered by this wave of verbal abuse, she felt only a sinking come over her. She panicked as it became obvious that nothing could be resolved there in that contention filled room and hurriedly excused herself to leave. Departing, she could hear them screaming at her.

The next few days were clouded over with "mists of darkness" and great, consuming depression. She wondered how she could have become so reckless, detached, and unfeeling in her life as to alienate these two sisters she loved so much. She began to plead to the Lord for forgiveness and mercy. She began to wonder if she was really loved for herself or was she just controlling others' love for her.

Her father came to try to comfort and reassure her. These daughters had come to him to solicit his support in confronting their sister. Instead, he had rebuked them and told them to look into their own eyes and remove the beam there first. He was sad to learn they had not heeded his counsel.

Her husband was also upset, realizing how they had invited her to the "court" without his knowledge or consent. He tried to console her. Comfort would not come. The words of her sisters, though mostly full of false accusation, contained just enough truth of the weaknesses she knew too well to make her doubt herself and her motivations.

Her father went back to each of his daughters and admonished them to right their wrong. He told them to search the scriptures and remove the beam from their eyes before

looking at the mote in another's. He was lovingly angry with
his daughters. He said that even if everything they had said
was true, she was not responsible for their happiness. They
were responsible for their own choices and that included
being happy.

One of the sisters opened her mind to the words of her father and the Spirit and softened. Her heart had been
touched. Her eyes were opened as she read in the Book of
Mormon that night, and the Lord spoke to her:

> And I exceedingly fear and tremble because of you, lest
> he shall suffer again; for behold, ye have accused him that he
> sought power and authority over you; but I know that he
> hath not sought for power nor authority over you, but he
> hath sought the glory of God, and your own eternal welfare.
>
> And ye have murmured because he hath been plain unto
> you. Ye say that he hath used sharpness; ye say that he hath
> been angry with you; but behold, his sharpness was the
> sharpness of the power of the word of God, which was in
> him; and that which ye call anger was the truth, according to
> that which is in God, which he could restrain, manifesting
> boldly concerning your iniquities. (2 Nephi 1:25–26.)

She humbly went to her sister and asked for forgiveness.
Tears were shed, love abounded, forgiveness ruled. Both were
comforted, renewed, replenished, and increased the power
and bond of their sisterhood. To this day, twenty years later,
the other sister remains a stranger, there is no communica-
tion and no relationship. She has for now relinquished the
bonds of an eternal relationship of sisterhood for the mental
stumbling block of pride.

And what of the father and daughter who found themselves in the middle of a serious conflict? They had always
been extremely close. Years of friendship had cemented an
eternal bond of kindredness. The father had sustained and
encouraged his daughter throughout her life, and now, in the

eventide of his life, she sought in return to give him the comforts of a peaceful life.

A very petty situation suddenly escalated until it became the center of a great conflict. Trying to resolve it, she wrote him a letter and struggled to explain her feelings. This attempt somehow backfired, and much to her amazement, she saw a strange side of her father manifest itself from an otherwise very humble spirit. She saw the ugly face of pride.

For days his countenance was changed. He was unwilling to talk. He preferred to defend and justify. He stubbornly exclaimed that he was going to move from the home they had provided for him, taking only his bed and books. His face showed the strain of pride's pain.

Concern for him grew to great worry. The daughter tried to reach him through love and patient discussion. She even approached him with the attitude of asking for his forgiveness for whatever she had done to offend him. She could only venture a guess as to why he had become so hostile and defensive. Perhaps some inner fear had been triggered by some unknown factor.

Two weeks passed without progress, and finally the daughter, having tried everything, pleaded with the Lord to help her. The thought immediately came to her, "you can reach your father through the scriptures." She arose from her knees and knew this was the right answer. She remembered her father loved the scriptures; he quoted them often. Her memories of him at home were of him stretched out across his bed lost in reading the scriptures.

But which scripture? Where would she find the one verse that would change his heart, soften his pride? She picked up the Book of Mormon and remembered the great contentions spoken of in the book of Helaman. She read: "And it came to pass that there arose a division among the people, insomuch that they divided hither and thither and went their ways, leaving Nephi alone, as he was standing in the midst of them. . . . And now it came to pass in the seventy and second year of the reign of the judges that the contentions did increase, insomuch that there were wars throughout all the land among all the people of Nephi." (Helaman 10:1, 11:1.)

She went, Book of Mormon in hand, to visit her father. She felt the Spirit rush over her as he opened the door. She told him of her prayer and she told him exactly what the Lord had said. Immediately, she could feel her father's humility return. Then, she said, "Dad, will you listen to these two scriptures as I substitute the word *family* for the words *people* and *land?*"

As she read the words, immediately he changed. His pride was melted to humility. She said, "Dad, even though whole nations were destroyed in the Book of Momon by contention, it still began in the heart of only one or two people. We cannot let that happen here."

The conflict was over. Embraces turned tension tender. Both could more clearly see a far greater field of vision.

What of the twenty-five-year-old mother of four who lacked self-confidence, felt untalented, and felt a lack of poise and ability to relate to others? She had been married at eighteen, straight from father's house to husband's house to motherhood. One baby after another and toddlers inbetween left little or no time for personal enrichment. She felt cheated out of a part of her youth. She felt uncomfortable and ill at ease around others who seemed more educated, more traveled, more well-spoken, well-groomed. She felt like a Freda Frump. She limited her social involvement with others because of her great discomfort in being around women who seemed more accomplished. This self-isolation only added to her lack of confidence.

During a conference talk given by President Ezra Taft Benson, who declared the value and charge to read the Book of Mormon, she felt the Spirit bear witness of the truth of his words. She resolved that night that she must find time to do this one thing, she had to, she knew it was her responsibility to do so, to hold to the rod.

At first she struggled with not only the time it took to read it, but also with the reading itself. She had not been much of a student in high school, and reading was slow for her. She had so many little ones and that meant strange and unpredictable hours each day. She seemed to always be tired. She struggled for weeks to implement this commitment into her daily routine. There was much frustration as she coped with the chaos of sick children, tantrums, late meals, dirty diapers, preschool activities, teething, and just the plain noise of family life and ever present, ever stepped-on, rarely picked up toys.

Finally, she decided one night that the laundry could wait until tomorrow. She picked up the scriptures and began again. Before she knew it, an hour had passed! She felt uplifted and knew with a surety right then that this quiet evening hour would suit her the best. A new commitment had begun, and from that day forth, those quiet, peaceful, twilight moments before the end of day, became her scripture study time. Sometimes it was minutes and sometimes it was an hour, but always she gave her full concentration.

As the weeks and months passed, she was surprised to find a little bud of new confidence beginning to bloom as she was able to answer questions in Gospel Doctrine class. She felt a sense of growing poise as she grew in her love of the Spirit she felt while she read. And then one night the Lord spoke to her as she read: "But behold, if ye will awake and arouse your faculties, even to an experiment upon my words, and exercise a particle of faith, yea, even if ye can no more than desire to believe, let this desire work in you, even until ye believe in a manner that ye can give place for a portion of my words" (Alma 32:27).

Here was the solution to her problems! She liked experiments, it was something she could see and feel. "Awake" (look, see, pay attention) and "arouse" (fill your heart with desire). She had a desire to believe she could be more friendly, more poised, more confident. The words *give place* meant to her to change, to change her attitude, especially toward herself.

She decided to stop feeling sorry for herself and to stop complaining that she had been cheated of her youth. After all, she had wanted this, it had been her choice at the time. Her youth was gone. This was her life now, she needed to make the best of it.

She also stopped saying and thinking about not being confident. She decided to "experiment" and just "act" as if she were confident. As she pushed herself to be more friendly, she became more friendly. She read the scriptures, she read other Church books. Her reading improved. She began to read novels and biographies. She completed reading the standard works. She used her knowledge in conversation with others. She became a teacher in Relief Society and grew in talents there.

Had she not told me this story I would never have guessed that she had once felt this way because she is one of the most friendly, confident, poised women I have ever met.

What of the parents who felt like failures when their oldest child turned his back on God, on the Church, on his family? The father blamed himself; he felt he had been too strict, perhaps he had made too many mistakes. The mother blamed herself; she felt she had been too lenient, she had made too many mistakes. They suffered. They wept. They tried to comfort one another. Finally, their suffering became so intense they could no longer console one another and so, each turned to the Lord for comfort and compassion.

The Lord spoke to the father first one night as he read: "And it came to pass that Laman and Lemuel and the sons of Ishmael did begin to murmur exceedingly, because of their sufferings and afflictions in the wilderness; and also my father began to murmur against the Lord his God; yea, and they were all exceedingly sorrowful, even that they did murmur against the Lord. Now it came to pass that I, Nephi, having been afflicted with my brethren because of the loss of my bow, and their bows having lost their springs, it began to be exceedingly difficult, yea, insomuch that we could obtain no food." (1 Nephi 16:20–23.)

He had forgotten that even Lehi, the prophet of God, had made a few mistakes too. Lehi had even murmured against God. He wondered if Lehi had even blamed himself for Laman and Lemuel not being faithful. He was certain that Lehi must have had his moments. But he began to see that in all his weakness Lehi had done the best he could. He began to remember all the family prayers, the family scripture study, the family home evenings, the ball games, the Scout trips, the camping trips, the ice cream floats, the bedtime stories, the hugs, the love. His heart began to pound as he felt new strength come into it. He had done his level best. He knew it. He could face the Lord. His child had his own agency. His child had chosen poorly. This father now knew he needed to pray with diligence and great love for the welfare of his child and turn him over to the Lord.

Within a short time his wife shared with him the moment the Lord had spoken to her when she read: "And now, because thou hast done this with such unwearyingness, behold, I will bless thee forever, and I will make thee mighty in word and in deed, in faith and in works; yea, even that all things shall be done unto thee according to thy word, for thou shalt not ask that which is contrary to my will" (Helaman 10:5).

Vibrant with enthusiasm and new strength, she told him that it occurred to her to put in the word *parenting* after *this*. She saw that this was the answer to their tormented prayer. They could pray with power and confidence, "even that all things shall be done" according to their word, because they had been unwearying in their parenting.

I have had similar experiences as I have turned to the scriptures and the Lord has spoken to me. One in particular stands out in my memory as a powerful witness that God speaks hope to his children so that we can truly see.

Concerned that one of my children who had experienced

repentance and then had fallen again, harder than ever, would never come back, the Lord spoke to me as I read: "Nevertheless, ye shall not cast him out of your synagogues, or your places of worship, for unto such shall ye continue to minister; for ye know not but what they will return and repent, and come unto me with full purpose of heart, and I shall heal them; and ye shall be the means of bringing salvation unto them" (3 Nephi 18:32). My places of worship are my heart, my home, my family. The message was clear, "never give up!"

What of the woman rejected by her family, scorned, borne false witness against, her own mother jealous of her? We don't think of these situations existing in families in the Church, but they do. All the members of this extended family are active members, but there is much contention and jealousy there.

One of the daughters has been rejected by several family members, including the mother. This sister spent years soliciting love from her mother. She struggled for years to overcome the underlying current of thought that if your mother doesn't love you, who could? At one point during the deepest struggles, this sister received an overwhelming reassurance from the Lord as he spoke to her when she read: "Is not this the carpenter, the son of Mary, the brother of James, and Joses, and of Juda, and Simon? and are not his sisters here with us? And they were offended at him. But Jesus said unto them, A prophet is not without honour, but in his own country, and among his own kin, and in his own house." (Mark 6:3–4.)

Even the Savior had been rejected by his own brothers and sisters. He really did know exactly how she felt. She could see that she would never be alone.

And what of the mission president who had to make a life-changing decision halfway through his mission?

He had come out into the mission field to serve three years for the Lord. He was a fabulously wealthy man with a large, successful business. Others would be at the helm for those three years. He was free to serve the Lord.

Halfway through his mission something happened in his company. Disaster seemed imminent. A decision had to be made. He needed to return and save his business or he would lose everything. Should he risk losing it all or stay and finish the work he had committed to do? The Lord spoke to him one night as he read: "And Jesus said unto him, No man, having put his hand to the plough, and looking back, is fit for the kingdom of God" (Luke 9:62).

That was all the decision there needed to be. He told his business managers to do the best they could, he would remain in this mission. For the next year his business hovered on the edge of complete failure. Crisis after crisis continued to be thrown in his way, but he never looked back, never allowed himself to be distracted. Then, a few months before he was to be released, the tide turned, a huge business deal became a success and the business became bigger than it was before he left.

And what of the young elder at the Missionary Training Center in Provo who wanted to go home because he had just learned his mother was dying in a hospital back home?

Many counseled with him, encouraging him to stay. Even his mother spoke to him by phone and told him in her weak and fragile voice that he was in the right place at the right time doing the right thing. Nevertheless, he could not be comforted. He wanted to go home.

He turned to the scriptures to look for direction. He wanted to go home, but he wanted to do the right thing. The Lord spoke to him as he read: "Therefore, thrust in your sickle with all your soul, and your sins are forgiven you, and you shall be laden with sheaves upon your back, for the laborer is worthy of his hire. Wherefore, your family shall live." (D&C 31:5.)

This young elder had enough faith to believe in every word the scriptures said of the direction he should go, so he told his mother he was staying and he knew she would live because he had a witness from the Lord. He completed his mission, married in the temple, and has several children. His mother is alive still today.

And what of the newly sustained stake Young Women president who was terrified of public speaking? She had a terrible experience as a teenager that had left her paralyzed with fear when called upon to even give a congregational prayer. She had even contemplated declining the position as she sat in the stake president's office because she felt so much anxiety over it.

But she knew that the Savior loved her, and if he wanted her to do this work, he would help her speak the words when she was called upon to do so.

It was shortly after her call that during her regular scripture study she came upon a verse from which she saw that her ability could increase: "Therefore, verily I say unto you, lift up your voices unto this people; speak the thoughts that I shall put into your hearts, and you shall not be confounded before men; for it shall be given you in the very hour, yea, in the very moment, what ye shall say. But a commandment I give unto you, that ye shall declare whatsoever thing ye declare in my name, in solemnity of heart, in the spirit of meekness, in all things. And I give unto you this promise, that inasmuch as ye do this the Holy Ghost shall be shed forth in bearing record unto all things whatsoever ye shall say." (D&C 100:5–8.)

This good sister lives in a fairly rural state, and today she is called upon to speak from chapel to chapel. Many are uplifted as her sweetness is reflected in her voice and countenance and the words of hope transcend heaven and earth.

What of the mother whose precious twelve-year-old son took his life by his own hand? She was a single parent. She had never married the boy's father. He had never known who his father was. His mother had been inactive during those years and had come back into activity when he was a small boy.

Being a single mother is hard. There are lots of lonely hours and never enough money. But they always had enough to get by. What she lacked in material goods she made up in love. Never was there a mother more devoted to her child. They were friends, they talked, they had a special bond.

There were no indications of anything wrong with her boy. He seemed a normal, happy, twelve year old, thrilled to become a deacon and receive the priesthood.

One evening they had a little argument and he stomped off to his room and slammed the door. The next morning when he didn't come to breakfast she assumed he had over-slept. When she opened his bedroom door, she opened a door to a personal hell, she discovered he had hung himself. Can you imagine her mist of darkness?

The official version was that he had probably been experi-menting and that it was an accident. But such a violent death with no real answers would leave a mother's heart riddled with pain, guilt, remorse, and blindness, especially since their last words had been cross ones.

The moment she walked through that door she entered a dark world of despair and doubt, overshadowed by her many past sins and poor choices. Her own life and past guilt now seemed to crush upon her in a way that even oxygen seemed to be a commodity she did not deserve.

Finally, nearly a year later, she began to pray again. Her prayers became sacred hours of soul searching; prayers of questions about her son. Then she began to pray for his salva-tion, for his rescue by the Savior. *Please, God,* she prayed, *he was only twelve years old. Please, God,* she wanted him to be happy. Could he be happy? She pleaded for his welfare, for his chance to have everything restored to him, to be able to be with him again someday. Sacred prayers from a broken-hearted mother. She began to read the scriptures again. She found herself being strengthened by daily feasting upon the words of Christ, and then the Lord spoke comfort to her and opened her eyes as she read: "Verily I say unto you my friends, fear not, let your hearts be comforted; yea, rejoice evermore, and in everything give thanks; waiting patiently on the Lord, for your prayers have entered into the ears of the Lord of Sabaoth, and are recorded with this seal and testament—the Lord hath sworn and decreed that they shall be granted. Therefore, he giveth this promise unto you, with an immutable covenant that they shall be fulfilled." (D&C 98:1–3.)

What of the man who had a goal to be a millionaire by the time he was twenty-eight? He passed up a mission because it would slow his progress toward his target date, he could not afford to give up the two years' time. He passed up Church callings, he worked many Sundays.

As his twenty-eighth birthday approached, it became clear he would not make his goal by that date. He set another target. He would have two million dollars by age thirty-five.

Then he met Debbie. She was a lovely Latter-day Saint woman, home from her mission about five years. They dated, and he fell madly in love. Debbie wasn't about to settle for less than a temple marriage, and she approached the relationship with caution. She had seen his careless attitude toward gospel priorities and she was concerned. She told him she would no longer date him because she wanted someone more committed.

This crushing news was a turning point for him. He had been rejected completely, something he had not been used to as he had pushed his way to his million-dollar goal. Suddenly, the goal of money paled to the feelings of his broken heart. He had seen reflected in Debbie's eyes the glimpse of the man he wanted, really wanted, to be.

He picked up his scriptures one evening, dusted them off, and began to read. Hours passed, and when he closed the book he had experienced an awakening. Early the next morning he opened them again and read the entire day. The hunger and thirst for knowledge and the Spirit consumed him. All these years he had neglected this nourishment. The Lord spoke to him when he read: "Think of your brethren like unto yourselves, and be familiar with all and free with your substance, that they may be rich like unto you. But before ye seek for riches, seek ye for the kingdom of God. And after ye have obtained a hope in Christ ye shall obtain riches, if ye seek them; and ye will seek them for the intent to do good—to clothe the naked, and to feed the hungry, and to liberate the captive, and administer relief to the sick and the afflicted." (Jacob 2:17–19.)

His priorities changed, and so his life changed. Today he is married in the temple (not to Debbie), a father of four, and very active in his ward and stake. Is he a millionaire? Perhaps, but that is not something he discusses. He would rather talk about the gospel.

What would have been the story, the outcome in all these people's lives had they not turned to the scriptures for knowledge? Eventually they may have ended up in the same place, but not without further delay and perhaps more suffering. We can say of these, "and they had waxed strong in the knowledge of the truth; for they were men [and women] of a sound understanding and they had searched the scriptures diligently, that they might know the word of God" (Alma 17:2).

Several years ago a book was published nationally, written by a Latter-day Saint dealing with a very sensitive subject. She implied in the book that the Church really offered no answers, no comfort, no concrete hope in this matter. She promoted a few anti-doctrine beliefs, such as hiring faith healers.

Soon after it was released I began receiving dozens of phone calls about my response to the book and its message. Looking back, I can see how my opinion became more militant with every phone call. I began to have unkind feelings towards the author.

It was during this time that I had a pressing obligation to speak to a large assembly of women. The preparation was not going well, I could not seem to put order to my thoughts. Finally, two days before the assignment, I humbled myself and pleaded to know where I might turn to find answers. The impression came to go to the Book of Mormon where, after a little page turning, my eyes fixed on these words: "See that ye are not lifted up unto pride; yea, see that ye do not boast in your own wisdom, nor of your much strength. Use boldness, but not overbearance; and also see that ye bridle all your passions, that ye may be filled with love; see that ye refrain from idleness. . . . Do not say: O God, I thank thee that we are better than our brethren; but rather say: O Lord, forgive my unworthiness, and remember my brethren in mercy—yea, acknowledge your unworthiness before God at all times." (Alma 38:11–12, 14.)

After some inner-vessel cleansing, I was able to return to my preparations, feel the Spirit influence me again, and feel love and kindness towards the author and my fellowmen.

Of equal impact on our vision is the word of God through his servants the prophets. How blessed we are to live in a dispensation when there is a living prophet on the earth! In a world filled with so much conflicting opinion, experts critiquing experts, and analysts by the hundreds on every theory, every event, offering every possible solution, it is a great comfort to know that there is a single, solid, steady voice of truth. That voice is the prophet and by extension the General Authorities of the Church. It may seem like a lone voice in a world of dispute, but it is not a voice alone. It is an echo of the very voice of God.

No matter how we see it, there is only one true view, and that is eternal perspective. Through eternal perspective, we can clearly see the rod and the road home. The prophet has the keys to that special lens of truth. His job is to keep the lens clearly and perfectly in focus, no matter what the pressures or ills against him may be.

Shortly after President Ezra Taft Benson was sustained as prophet, he held a special fireside for all parents in the Church. During this inspired message he called upon all the mothers to come home from the workplace. He spoke of his concern for the children, for the marriages, for the safety of the Saints because mothers were absent from the home.

For the better part of the following year, whenever I had a speaking assignment, I was asked if I would address President Benson's "controversial talk." Evidently it had sent a wave of debate throughout the Church. I was asked to express my opinion because I had a career. People were curious as to how I was dealing with this matter.

My remarks about his message were always brief and I always began with this sentence: "I have been asked to comment on what was described to me as 'President Benson's controversial talk.' Let me first say that in no way was President Benson's talk controversial. He is the prophet of God, and a prophet has spoken. Our attitude toward his talk is the only thing that seems to me to be controversial."

Then, I explained that my experience has been that when I bark the loudest, I am usually in the wrong. Our responsibility is to seek the Lord's will. The prophet counsels us as if the Lord himself were present.

The prophet doesn't know our individual circumstances, some situations are desperate, others may be unlike anything we expect. I encouraged the sisters to pay attention to their hearts. If we are troubled and confused and not at peace it usually means we are in the wrong place. We each have the same opportunity to take our decisions to the Lord.

We all know what it feels like to have great unrest in our bosoms. This is our gift; to feel after the spiritual responsibilities of one another and ourselves. The Lord uses that special endowment of the heart to feel what our spiritual responsibilities are. I have found it impossible to live day after day with unrest in my heart. When such times have happened, I have had to first examine my circumstance, my attitude, my choices, and then go to the Lord. This was especially true once when I fought the feelings that I should have another baby and also true when I had made an issue over the "principle of the thing" with someone. And also true when I asked the Lord about my career after making a decision to quit.

Whatever the prophet counsels and warns is from the Lord, and we must not find that controversial. We have the privilege of direct revelation for instruction in each of our lives in holding fast to the rod. We know when we are in the wrong place at the wrong time doing the wrong thing, no matter what that is, sins of commission or sins of omission. Our hearts really do tell us that.

Hardening our hearts causes blindness. When we become too concerned with looking inward we will be unable to see the prophet pointing the way home.

There is an old proverb that goes something like this: "The best mirror you will ever have is the face of a friend."

What better friend do we have than the Savior? His image and his being and his voice are in the scriptures. The scriptures are the Urim and Thummim for us to see the road to the Savior. They are the rod along the road to the celestial kingdom. They are a mirror, indeed, the best mirror we will ever have. Not only do we look into them to see eternal perspective, but they also reflect back to us our worth and our goodness.

"Search the scriptures; for in them ye think [remember] ye have eternal life" (John 5:39).

There are those who although they believe in Jesus Christ, do not believe him when he, through the voice of his prophets, instructs us as to all things we must do to inherit the celestial kingdom. Whether that voice is through the scriptures or from latter-day prophets, both living and dead, we are responsible to accept and follow that instruction.

"And now remember, remember, my brethren, that whosoever perisheth, perisheth unto himself; and whosoever doeth iniquity, doeth it unto himself; for behold, ye are free; ye are permitted to act for yourselves; for behold, God hath given unto you a knowledge and he hath made you free" (Helaman 14:30).

We are free to *remember* . . . and perish not.

5

ALWAYS REMEMBER HIM

*That they are willing to take
upon them the name of thy son,
and always remember him and
keep his commandments which he
has given them; that they may
always have his Spirit to be with them.*
—D&C 20:77

*H*aving and keeping eternal perspective is one of life's truly tedious efforts. It is often the most difficult part of a trial. Often, it would be far easier to endure the actual moments of pain if we could see the larger picture, if we could see much farther than mortal view. The lack of eternal perspective is more painful to endure at times, than the trial itself.

Many years ago I knew a couple who were prominent, active members in the ward and stake. The wife was always involved in serving others. Her husband held a significant stake position and was equally service oriented. It was a complete shock when the wife revealed to me her recent discovery of her husband's numerous adulterous affairs and addiction to pornography. I could not understand how this could have happened. Of course there must have been deep problems he never dealt with. I am sure psychologists would be able to fill the pages of this book with all the reasons for his problems.

But, over the years as I have pondered his situation and many more like it, it seems to me that when we lack eternal perspective we are more easily persuaded to let go of the rod.

Eternal perspective is the larger picture. It is "picturing ourselves" where we came from, why we are here, and where we are going. It is "imagining" ourselves dressed in white, standing in the hallways of heaven.

It is believing Christ when he says he can save us. It is imagining ourselves as gods, working together, male and female, husbands, wives, brothers, sisters, gods together creating and co-creating worlds without end.

Eternal perspective is remembering. It is also pondering, thinking, considering, looking forward, and imagining.

Looking forward, imagining ourselves as gods, in God's presence, is eternal perspective.

"Do you *look forward* with an eye of faith and view this mortal body raised in immortality, and this corruption raised in incorruption? . . . Can you *imagine* to yourselves that ye hear the voice of the Lord, saying unto you, in that day: Come unto me ye blessed, for behold, your works have been the works of righteousness upon the face of the earth?" (Alma 5:15–16; emphasis added.)

The message is to see and look forward to him who is leading us. Look forward, not backwards, the Savior is up ahead, leading us to the celestial kingdom; he knows the way.

"See that ye take care of these sacred things, yea, see that ye look to God and live" (Alma 37:47).

The message is to see and look up to Christ and "let us remember him, and lay aside our sins and not hang down our heads . . . for we are not cast off" (2 Nephi 10:20).

The message is to "cast about your eyes and begin to believe in the son of God, that he will come to redeem his people . . . and die to atone for their sins" (Alma 33:22).

The message is to see and to "look forward unto Christ with steadfastness," and we will be among "they which shall not perish" (2 Nephi 26:8).

Do we remember when the Lord sent fiery flying serpents among the Israelites to soften their hardened hearts? And after he did this he "prepared a way that they might be healed; and the labor they had to perform was to look." But, because this was so simple many didn't place any value on the invitation and "there were many who perished" (1 Nephi 17:41). But, "whosoever would look upon it might live. And many did look and live." (Alma 33:19.)

Do we remember when Moroni tore off a piece of his coat and wrote upon it, "In memory of our God, our religion, and freedom, and our peace, our wives, and our children"? Then he hoisted it upon the end of a pole and "poured out his soul to God." And then he "went forth among the people, waving the rent part of his garment in the air, that all might see the writing which he had written." (Alma 46:12–19.) He wanted them to remember their covenants and always look to Christ and live!

Do we remember the two thousand sons of Helaman, otherwise called the Stripling Warriors? They had not taken the oath to never bear arms like their fathers had and stepped forward valiantly to defend the liberty of their families, friends, and the right to worship their God. They were young and had never "fought, yet they did not fear death" (Alma 56:47). We could easily say that their fearlessness was the folly of youth who deem themselves invincible anyway. Or we could declare it as the idealism of crusading youth who always seem to be on one battlefront or another.

But this was not the case. "They did think more upon the liberty of their fathers . . . ; they had been taught by their mothers, that if they did not doubt, God would deliver them. And they rehearsed [*remembered*] unto me the words of their mothers, saying: We do not doubt our mothers knew it." (Alma 56:47–48.)

They remembered the words of their mothers who certainly did "talk of Christ, . . . rejoice in Christ, . . . preach of Christ, . . . prophesy of Christ . . . that [their] children may know to what source to look for a remission of their sins. . . . [And] may look forward unto that life which is in Christ." (2 Nephi 25:26–27.)

Do we remember the terrified and shaken people of Nephi, gathered in sorrow and wonderment, after three days of earthquakes, thunder, lightning, tempest, and whirlwinds; even a "great and terrible destruction"? (3 Nephi 8:12.) Highways were gone, mountains leveled, cities sunk or burned, death and carnage everywhere.

These people stood near the temple in the land Bountiful discussing these events and "wondering with one another." And "while they were thus conversing one with another, they heard a voice as if it came out of heaven; and they cast their eyes round about, for they understood not the voice which they heard" (3 Nephi 11:3).

A second time the voice spoke, again, they looked around and did not understand what was said or what was happening.

A third time they heard the voice, and this time, "did open their ears to hear it; and their eyes were towards the sound thereof; and they did *look* steadfastly towards heaven, from whence the sound came" (3 Nephi 11:5; emphasis added).

This time they understood the voice. They witnessed the Savior descend before them and were able to participate in the marvelous witness that he is Jesus Christ, the Son of God.

The message is to look, look up, look up to Christ, and imagine ourselves with him. We look with our spiritual eyes so that we will always remember him.

Peter was in the storm-tossed boat the night the Savior came towards them upon the water. He looked up and saw the Savior and heard his voice, "Be of good cheer; it is I; be not afraid" (Matthew 14:27). Peter looked up—he walked out upon the raging waters—but then, something happened: he looked away, he looked down, he looked around, "but when he saw the wind boisterous, he was afraid," and he sank (Matthew 14:30). The message is *look up,* look up during the trials and stormy seas of affliction to the Savior and always re-member him.

Remember when Mary came upon the empty tomb? She inquired as to where they had taken Jesus. She supposed someone had taken him, but she knew not where and then "she turned herself back, and saw Jesus standing, and knew not that it was Jesus" (John 20:14).

In tears she answered his question as to why she was weeping—she thought he was the gardener. She asked him where Jesus had been taken to which he responded by calling her name, then she looked up and saw the Savior (see John 20:16).

The message is, be still, don't murmur so that we can hear our name, and look up.

The Apostle Stephen boldly declared repentance to the Sanhedrin and "they were cut to the heart." They "gnashed on him with their teeth" and condemned him to death by stoning (Acts 7:54). But Stephen "looked up stedfastly into heaven, and saw the glory of God, and Jesus standing on the right hand of God. . . . And they stoned Stephen, calling upon God, and saying, Lord Jesus, receive my spirit." (Acts 7:55, 59.)

If we but look up to the Savior and always remember him we can have eternal perspective in the midst of sore trials and endure to the end.

Joseph Smith related a vision he had while praying for the main body of the Quorum of Twelve Apostles who were on foreign shores trying to proselyte the gospel. They had returned one evening to their dwelling, tired, discouraged, disheartened, and darkened. They stood in a circle, their heads hung low, their clothes worn, their feet swollen, their eyes cast downward. Joseph Smith saw them in vision in this condition and then saw the Savior descending above them, standing just above their heads (see *History of the Church,* 2:381). Joseph knew the Savior was waiting for them to look up, he alone could offer the comfort they needed, but they did not see him because they would not look up.

I know of a handicapped runner in a city's marathon race. He was horribly crippled and limited in his abilities, but he was determined to enter, participate, and finish. His efforts were remarkable. But to me, even more remarkable were the two spectators that remained in the drizzling rain long after the crowds dispersed, long after the last runners had come in, hour after hour, waiting for him to finish. As he turned for the final stretch he felt as if his lungs would burst and his muscles collapse if he even took one more step. Even with the knowledge that it was the final mile he still seemed to be drained of his last shred of strength. Then, he looked up, he saw those two spectators, cheering for him, and felt their love and commitment for him, and was strengthened by that love and commitment and finished the race.

Those two spectators were his parents, not unlike our heavenly parents and the Savior who are there for us, hour after hour, waiting for us to finish, lending their love and support, if we but look up. The message is, look up. Don't give up on our spiritually handicapped loved ones, don't give up on the Lord, don't give up on ourselves, look up to the Savior and finish the course.

My stake president has related a tender moment when he was a bishop and had to preside over the funeral of a young child in his ward. Shortly before the service, he went into the Relief Society room as they were about to close the casket. The parents had been given a few last moments alone with their precious little one. As he solemnly approached, the mother began to speak. "Bishop, I have two other children with this same disease and they are going to die as well, but I can make it, Bishop. I felt the Savior here, I looked up, I didn't see him, but I tell you, he was in here with me today, and I felt his arms around me."

The message is, look up to the Savior and always remember him. We can have eternal perspective in the midst of our sorrows, and that perspective can help us endure to the end.

I testify that there are and have been and will continue to

be many occasions in our lives where we will have the opportunity to look up and see the Savior and know that he is there.
Although we may not really see him in personage, we will
know with assurety that he was with us that day and that he is
leading us home!

The message is to look up. Even as Christ was *lifted up*, if
we will look up upon him with spiritual eyes for the direction
we should go, we can be healed. Even in our suffering for sin
and sorrows, even during our efforts to repent, we can have
eternal perspective and not perish in a sea of worthlessness
and tribulation. "Yea, see that ye look to God and live" (Alma
37:47).

The Savior's example of looking up should inspire us to
always remember him as we seek to maintain eternal perspective amidst our conflict and trial of this, our one and only
wilderness experience.

"And it came to pass, when the time was come that he
should be received up, he stedfastly set his face to go to
Jerusalem" (Luke 9:51).

This was his wilderness experience. He went the full measure of sacrifice in order to be The Exemplar, in order to be
able to lead us safely home. If we, too, but look up and steadfastly set our faces towards him, we can be healed and live
eternally with him. "And I will also be your light in the wilderness; and I will prepare the way before you, if it so be that ye
shall keep my commandments; wherefore, inasmuch as ye
shall keep my commandments ye shall be led towards the
promised land; and ye shall know that it is by me that ye are
led" (1 Nephi 17:13).

"And whoso receiveth you, there I will be also, for I will go
before your face. I will be on your right hand and on your
left, and my Spirit shall be in your hearts, and mine angels
round about you, to bear you up." (D&C 84:88.)

"And now, my son, I trust that I shall have great joy in you,
because of your steadiness and your faithfulness unto God;
for as you have commenced in your youth to look to the Lord

your God, even so I hope that you will continue in keeping his commandments; for blessed is he that endureth to the end" (Alma 38:2).

As we make this great effort to endure to the end with eyes fixed on the Lord, it is important for us to remember that we have to have our minds on our work. That work also includes carpools, jobs, laundry, food preparation and consumption, meetings, childbearing and rearing and maintenance, husband and wife negotiations, calorie counting, maid service, and all other needed worldly repairs!

We need to have fun in this life and enjoy the good things of the earth. One way we always remember him is to enjoy what he has given us and thank him constantly for it!

> The fulness of the earth is yours, the beasts of the field and the fowls of the air, and that which climbeth upon the trees and walketh upon the earth;
>
> Yea, and the herb, and the good things which come of the earth, whether for food or for raiment, or for houses, or for barns, or for orchards, or for gardens, or for vineyards;
>
> Yea, all things which come of the earth, in the season thereof, are made for the benefit and the use of man, both to please the eye and to gladden the heart;
>
> Yea, for food and for raiment, for taste and for smell, to strengthen the body and to enliven the soul.
>
> And it pleaseth God that he hath given all these things unto man; for unto this end were they made to be used, with judgment, not to excess, neither by extortion. (D&C 59:16–20.)

In other words, the Lord wants us to enjoy our wallpaper, our construction paper, our newspaper, our term paper, and our wrapping paper! He wants us to enjoy our ice cream, our sour cream, and our cold cream! He wants us to enjoy our Church books, our music books, our textbooks, our cookbooks, our coloring books, and our storybooks. He wants us to enjoy our clothes and hose, our flats and hats, our rings and things, "to please the eye and to gladden the heart . . . and to enliven the soul."

He wants us to have joy and enjoyment in this world. "And it pleaseth God that he hath given all these things unto man; for unto this end were they made to be used, with judgment, not to excess, neither by extortion" (D&C 59:20).

This is a telestial world, and we have telestial bodies. They get tired, sick, and flabby. Our spirits learn to be submissive to the Spirit. We are continually renewed and refreshed when we follow celestial standards.

But we live here in the world! And the work here is a lot of "stuff" we need to learn to enjoy.

"Come, follow me" is the counsel. He didn't say we have to walk beside him or ahead of him, but follow him.

We all make mistakes, even on a daily basis. It's part of the process. We all have temptations. Temptations in and of themselves are not sins. But when we act on those temptations and let them control us, then we sin.

Tough times are here. Tougher ones are coming. Now is no time to massage past grievances or lick old wounds, self-inflicted or otherwise. Maybe now is even the time for an ego enema or two.

Humility and gratitude are needed to always remember him and prevent perishing. Humility and gratitude nurture eternal perspective. The more we look up to the Savior, the more we begin to see him in all things. "And all things which have been given of God from the beginning of the world, unto man, are the typifying of him" (2 Nephi 11:4).

As we deepen our appreciation of the Savior—his goodness to us, his sacrifice for us—our eternal perspective deepens and expands. Trials become more bearable, and we find greater joy in the ordinary mundane parts of life.

A member of my stake, an educator, tells how his father always taught him in parables. He had grown up in a small, rural town where the local veterinarian had a sign over his shop that read:

VETERINARIAN/TAXIDERMIST

and underneath in small print were the words:

EITHER WAY YOU GET YOUR DOG BACK.

His father was trying to teach him that it is up to each of us to develop a proper perspective of life. Whatever happens to us, we know we can make the best of it. If we are without joy in this life, it is because we, ourselves, have not allowed ourselves to be joyful. Even if we are locked within prison walls, persecuted, abandoned, spat upon, or neglected by others, we can choose. The gospel perspective teaches us to have joy as we live in a telestial world, struggling to overcome it.

When this same good brother began his career as a teacher he was assigned to intern with a kindergarten class somewhere in Scottsdale, Arizona. On the first day, as he entered the classroom, the children were dancing in a circle as the teacher played the piano. As each little child took his seat, one little boy kept dancing, obviously full of great joy. This new teacher went over and said to the little boy, "Well, you really like to dance don't you?"

The little boy looked up at him, very puzzled and said, "No, I don't like to dance." Then pointing to his teacher he said, "She likes me to!" He had decided to have joy in his experience.

If we fail to look forward, impatiently waiting for a trying circumstance to end, or worse, if we are continually waiting to arrive at perfection, we will miss the best parts of life!

There should be joy in the striving as well as in the arriving.

With all the mounting wickedness in the world we do get discouraged, especially as that wickedness brushes against us, even as we do hand-to-hand combat with the adversary.

But we cannot forget that our heavenly parents are successful parents, and many of their children, "so great a multitude which no man could number," are going to make it all the way across this wilderness back home to them. When you consider that our heavenly parents must endure more than we in our trials as they watch the suffering of their children, knowing they have power to end it, doesn't it make eternal perspective become more precious to grasp and understand? There must be an incredible view from where they sit.

This world of turmoil requires telestial stretching toward celestial marks. It is the direction of the stretch that is worth pondering. There isn't one of us that right now can't look back and say that in some form or another at some time in our lives: "I have grown." And looking back at the growth, the direction has been to what? I believe it has been toward the Savior, looking up, becoming more like Christ. If we can cease our murmuring and settle it once and for all in our hearts to "always remember him" (Moroni 4:3), then, even a year from now we can look up and once again say, "I can't believe how much I've grown!"

The message is look up to the Savior and always remember him.

It was Easter Sunday 1992, the most memorable Easter of my life, although it didn't begin that way.

We woke up that morning in Salzburg, Austria. We had been visiting our daughter who had been studying in London. The whole family was together for a holiday, and this was our last day together. We had to return to Munich, Germany, about a three hour drive, in order for Ashley to get a plane back to school and for us to return home.

When we arrived in Munich we discovered that we had been misinformed. We had missed the American sacrament meeting, and no one could help us find another. We had tried for several hours and finally realized that most meetings were probably over.

We discussed various things we could do that day that would be appropriate and in accordance with keeping the Sabbath holy. The almost unanimous vote was to go to the concentration camp, Dachau, located twenty minutes outside of Munich. I cast the one dissenting vote.

I had heard stories of the sad spirit there and the depressing mood. This was Easter, and it was our last day together. I didn't want to end this wonderful trip with such a dreary experience. I protested again. But my family insisted. Besides, this was history. This was a once in a lifetime chance to understand the Holocaust. We went to Dachau.

From the moment we stepped through the fence we felt the sadness engulf us like a black mist. Even my youngest, then nine years old, noticed it. People were leaving with moist eyes. There was a hush, and an overwhelming feeling of emptiness. I felt we had made a terrible mistake coming here. Little did I know that it was going to be a great Easter Sunday.

We entered the photo museum; old officer's barracks preserved to hold a pictorial essay of the beginning of the Third Reich, the conception of concentration camps, and the history of Dachau. We began in a room with small photos, and as we moved from room to room the photos became larger and larger and more and more grotesque until finally we were staring face to face at the worst atrocities man could inflict upon his brothers and sisters.

We were sickened. At one point I left the buildings, finally overcome with alternating feelings of nausea and utter sadness. I had had enough. My heart was heavy. I was sure that we had come to the wrong place that day.

My family wanted to see the movie on the history of the camp. The English version was to play in thirty minutes, time enough to walk the compound and go to the ovens. I told them I would go to the ovens, but I wasn't going to the movie.

As we approached the separate area with the gas chamber showers and ovens, my children grew more amazed. We all entered one building, and at that point even they didn't want to see much more. The sadness we felt was real and getting more oppressive by the moment.

Again I declined the movie. This time my husband put his arm around me and suggested that I go in, close my eyes, but listen. This was, indeed, a once in a lifetime experience, something we would never choose to do again, but something we would ponder for the rest of our lives. It was important to remember these things. I knew he was right and I felt a sweet spirit inspire me to go in and listen.

The lights went out, and I closed my eyes. The narrator began to describe the early days of Dachau and then he moved on to the conditions of the war and then to the conditions of the prisoners. He described events that led to the disease, devastation, starvation, and death, and senseless slaughter of so many. He told the statistics, and then, he said something that transformed that day from one of sadness to one of joy.

He said that although many died in Dachau of disease, genocide, and starvation, many more would have died except for one thing, *brotherly kindness.* Even though the stories were few of those who shared their crust of bread or gave away their newspapers so another could stuff their clothes and keep out the cold, those few gave renewed hope to many. Those few who had brotherly kindness saved many with love and hope.

The miracle for me had happened. As he said the words, "brother kindness," a sudden intelligence flowed through me. I recognized at once that even in this house of endless hours of horror where there was so much despair, that brotherly kindness was possible because of one thing, the Atonement! That in Gethsemane, in another hour of sorrows, the Savior suffered it all, even "he suffereth the pains of all men, yea, the pains of every living creature, both men, women, and children, who belong to the family of Adam" (2 Nephi 9:21) "that the word might be fulfilled which saith he will take upon him the pains and the sicknesses of his people" (Alma 7:11).

In Gethsemane the Savior knew and bore the sorrows of Dachau.

In that dark room, my eyes tightly shut, I saw the brilliant light of the Atonement! The Savior came across eternity to succor those souls in Dachau.

I believe there will never be a place on the face of the earth where oppression will quench even a flicker of hope. The Savior is always there. Brotherly kindness was possible, even if in the hearts of only a few, because the Savior sustained those people. He came across eternity with his peace and power and hope, even to a people who didn't believe in him!

It was a glorious Easter Sunday after all!

The word *remember* is precious to the Lord. He brings it to our thoughts twice each week. Every Sunday we mentally renew covenants as we partake of sacramental emblems that we may "always remember him," and look up to the Savior remembering to "keep his commandments . . . that [we] may always have his Spirit to be with [us]" (Moroni 4:3).

And is not a covenant a two-way promise? Will he remember us?

"Can a woman forget her suckling child? . . . yet will I not forget thee. Behold, I have graven thee upon the palms of my hands." (Isaiah 49:15–16.)

President David O. McKay related a dream: "I then fell asleep, and beheld in vision something infinitely sublime. In the distance I beheld a beautiful white city. Though far away, yet I seemed to realize that trees with luscious fruit, shrubbery with gorgeously-tinted leaves, and flowers in perfect bloom abounded everywhere." (Clare Middlemiss, *Cherished Experiences from the Writings of David O. McKay* [Salt Lake City: Deseret Book Co., 1965], p. 109.)

Then he saw a great concourse of people approaching the city, each one wearing a flowing white headdress and robe. They were being led by a man that President McKay, although only discerning the profile of his face and body, recognized at once as the Savior. He described his countenance and radiating peace as sublime and divine! Somehow he understood that city was the Savior's—The City Eternal—and the people who were following him were going to abide there in peace and eternal joy.

President McKay wondered who these people were. It seemed that the Savior could read President McKay's thoughts; He stopped and pointed to a semicircle that appeared above them. President McKay looked up, written in gold were the words:

"These are they who have overcome the world, who truly have been born again."

The best mirror we'll ever have is the face of our friend, Jesus Christ. And what will it reflect? "Can ye look up to God at that day with a pure heart and clean hands? . . . Can you look up, having the image of God engraven upon your countenances?" (Alma 5:19.)

I think you can because you are also my mirror. And when I look into your great and noble faces, so earnestly seeking to do God's will, I see some of my own worth reflected in your image. Can you ever know how much that has meant to me in my life and continues to matter so much?

In times of discouragement, often, I have looked up and seen one of you with the face of the Savior upon your countenance and once again I have known of his redeeming love.

Fifteen years ago I read an article written by someone who professed that the members of the Church could be divided into two groups. He said one group in the Church are those who are led by blind faith, they will do whatever they are told to do, never questioning. This group he called the Iron Rods. They don't question, but they don't think either. They just go along and respond. The second group were called free thinkers, those who eventually do what is asked, but they will question and seek their own verification by the Spirit. He called this group the Liahonas.

About eight years later a good friend brought me this same article thinking that I might enjoy reading it. I recognized the title and realized it was the same one I had read years earlier. I almost was ready to decline reading it again until he said, "I thought you would like it. You will see, too, that you are definitely an Iron Rod." This was what caused me to want to reread it. Eight years earlier I remembered distinctly believing I was a Liahona! It intrigued me, what had changed? What was it this friend saw differently in me now?

Several hours later as I began the first paragraph of the article I found myself confused, bewildered, and struggling with the philosophy. I could no longer see myself as either an Iron Rod or a Liahona, according to his description. What was it? What was different? Why was this now causing me so much confusion?

Thinking upon the relationship I felt now with the Church and with the Lord, I began to realize that this article contained knowledge, but it lacked spiritual wisdom. The issue for us as members is not one of free thinking or blind faith. Rather, the focus for each of us is, how can I be of one heart and one mind with Jesus Christ?

We continue to make our lives more difficult, more complicated, more full of risk if we try to struggle through life on our will alone. "For behold, it is as easy to give heed to the word of Christ, which will point to you a straight course to eternal bliss, as it was for our fathers to give heed to this compass, which would point unto them a straight course to the promised land. And now I say, is there not a type in this thing? For just as surely as this director did bring our fathers, by following its course, to the promised land, shall the words of Christ, if we follow their course, carry us beyond this vale of sorrow into a far better land of promise." (Alma 37:44–45.)

The Savior asked us to take his yoke, "For my yoke is easy, and my burden is light" (Matthew 11:30). In other words, if we remember the Savior and the Atonement and what and why he sacrificed for us, we will earnestly desire to keep the commandments. Keeping the commandments suddenly becomes easy. We then realize that keeping the commandments has always been easy. The task of keeping the commandments is lighter than the burden of unkept promises and unresolved sins. Sins of commission or omission each bring with them their unique but equally and heavy burdens. What a relief to obey, to yoke ourselves to the Lord, to let him help us pull the load. His yoke is easy. It is much easier to keep the commandments than to be weighed down with the pain, sorrow, deceit, guilt, loneliness, and despair that disobedience brings.

You and I cannot become perfect without the Savior. We can't *make ourselves* sinless because we are already full of sin, aren't we? We will likely live out our mortal lives in this cycle of sinning and struggling to overcome sin. Then what hope do we have of—do we dare say it?—becoming like Christ? How can we be assured of our place in the celestial kingdom when we can't even be sure tomorrow will be a sinless day for us?

In the Doctrine and Covenants is recorded a small description of those who will inherit the celestial kingdom. It is brief, but it is perhaps the most hopeful piece of doctrine taught to man. "These are they whose names are written in heaven, where God and Christ are the judge of all. These are they who are just men made perfect through Jesus the mediator of the new covenant, who wrought out this perfect atonement through the shedding of his own blood." (D&C 76: 68–69.)

It doesn't say "these are they who are perfect." It says clearly, *"just men made perfect through Jesus."* And that is the great hope we have and the great gift of the Atonement in our lives!

The Savior can truly, literally, save us, "after all we can do" for ourselves (2 Nephi 25:23). What does "after all we can do" mean? Does that mean I should take one commandment at a time and live it to perfection and then go on to the next one and master that and on and on until I become perfect?

Stephen E. Robinson in his book, *Believing Christ,* reminds us that the Apostle Paul pointed out that the idea of trying to keep all the commandments is very different from actually keeping them. Paul clearly shows us that to rely on our own ability to keep all the commandments makes the atonement of Christ ineffectual in our lives (see Galations 5:4). Brother Robinson teaches that "we can't earn our way into the celestial kingdom by keeping all the commandments. We could in theory, but we can't in practice—because neither you nor I nor anybody else has kept *all* the commandments." (*Believing Christ* [Salt Lake City: Deseret Book Co., 1992], p. 42.)

Brother Robinson explains that it is impossible for us to do so because of our fallen states, therefore a merciful God has provided us with a covenant we can keep. "Jesus Christ is the one who redeems us from the curse of the law—from the demand for perfect performance—by offering a new means of justification, not by law (keeping all the rules all the time), but by faith in Christ" (p. 41).

You have heard it said that we can only count on two things: death and taxes. In this world of confusion, conflicting expert opinion, and hypocrisy, there really does seem to be very little we can count on.

But I have a growing list of hope. I can count on the prophet to never lead me away from the iron rod. I can count on the Holy Ghost to warn me, counsel me, teach me, inspire me, comfort me, chastise me, draw me to repentance, and reveal to me all things I must do. I can count on the love of my husband and children to sustain me, and more. I can count on the love of God for me, no matter how little he can count on me. And I can count on you. I can count on that feeling, nurturing, spiritual endowment you have to reach out for spiritual responsibilities. I can count on you to help me change some spiritual tires that go flat from time to time. I can surely, truly, count on this "vast community of believers" that forever binds you and me and all the sons and daughters of God together in this world and in the one to come!

And, finally, I can count on the Atonement. I can *"remember"* what the Lord has done for me, yea, even that he hath heard my prayer; yea, then do I remember his merciful arm which he extendeth towards me" (Alma 29:10; emphasis added).

A sister from our ward recently returned from her mission and shared with us the story of a teenage girl, who, after investigating the Church had received a powerful witness of it's truth and desired baptism. Her mother granted permission with no hesitation. When she approached her father, however, he was not so eager and expressed his deep concern. He told her she could do this if she wanted to, but if she did, this would be the biggest disappointment of his life.

This young woman struggled with her decision for days. She discussed it with no one because her heart was heavy with concern for her father. She felt a burden beyond her ability to comprehend. She did not want to disappoint her father.

Finally, one day at school, she found an opportunity to share her dilemma with a fourteen-year-old boy from the ward. This young teacher listened with empathy as she poured out her heart regarding her love for the gospel, her knowledge of it's truth, and her father's warning.

He listened patiently. And then, in a voice of wisdom far beyond his years, he simply asked her one question: "Well, which father would you rather disappoint?"

She was baptized the next weekend.

I don't know her name, but I am thankful for the example she was.

Those most interested in the remains of a lost soldier are not his math teacher, Church leader, coach, or boss. Those who are relentless in that search for the missing man are the parents, the wife, children, and brothers and sisters.

The Savior wants us, his family, home. He is the most interested in our return. He suffered, he literally, truly suffered that he might help us bear our burdens and be able to redeem us. He, with open heart and open arms, declares:

"Look unto me, and endure to the end, and ye shall live; for unto him that endureth to the end will I give eternal life" (3 Nephi 15:9).

Here we walk, you and I, among the jagged rocks of an uphill path that runs alongside that sturdy rod of iron. We hold fast, blindly groping through mists of difficulties and disappointments. We cannot see most of the time the way ahead, so we listen. We can hear many voices calling, tempting us away from the rod: voices of pleasure and voices of worldly gain. And we can feel the winds of change press fiercely against us.

But listen again, listen carefully. Do you hear it? Above the murmuring crowd do you hear another voice? Soft, steady, ever strong: "Come, listen to a prophet's voice, and hear the word of God" (*Hymns,* no. 21).

And as we walk, clinging with calloused hands, to the iron rod, every now and then we catch a glimpse of where we are going. Every now and then we see ourselves, the person who awaits us, the person we really want to be. We see ourselves every time we kneel at temple altars, or hold our newborns in our arms, or soothe a broken heart, or say I'm sorry, or lift another's burdens, or protect and teach a small child, or during countless other acts of love and service given with no thought to ourselves. We then see the goodness in ourselves. We know it is there. We want more of it. We hold on tighter and keep walking, as tedious as the journey may seem at times.

And there is more, much more. In these glimpses, every now and then, we look up and see him, the Savior who awaits us, who is saving us, cheering us on. We hear him every time we hear the prophets or when we read their messages or when we read the scriptures or when in repentance and prayer we are inspired.

Holding fast, listen again, listen carefully. Do you hear it above the murmuring crowd? "My name is Jehovah, and I know the end from the beginning; therefore my hand shall be over thee" (Abraham 2:8). "Be of good cheer, for I will lead you along" (D&C 78:18).

INDEX